South Asia's Integration into the World Economy

Miria Pigato, Caroline Farah, Ken Itakura
Kwang Jun, Will Martin, Kim Murrell,
and T. G. Srinivasan

The World Bank
Washington, D.C.

The opinions expressed in this report do not necessarily represent the views of the World Bank or its member governments. The World Bank does not guarantee the accuracy of the data included in this publication and accepts no responsibility whatsoever for any consequence of their use. The boundaries, colors, denominations, and other information shown on any map in this volume do not imply on the part of the World Bank Group any judgment on the legal status of any territory or the endorsement or acceptance of such boundaries.

Cover photos (all from the World Bank): Women picking tea leaves in Sri Lanka, by Yosef Hadar (top left); female inspector at HES Ltd., an alarm and electric clock part manufacturer in India, by Ray Witlin (top right); electric power lines in India, by Curt Carnemark (bottom left); and worker surveying a construction area, Tarbela, Pakistan, by Tomas Sennett (bottom right).

ISBN: 0-8213-4039-5

This report was prepared by a team drawn from the Prospects and Research Groups, Development Economics, The World Bank. The team was lead by Miria Pigato and comprised Caroline Farah, Ken Itakura, Kwang Jun, Will Martin, Kim Murrell, and T. G. Srinivasan, working under the guidance of Uri Dadush. Sara Crow and Chi Ezenwa provided production assistance.

CONTENTS

FOREWORD

One of the historic shifts in thinking in the field of development economics over the past quarter century has been the change in views on foreign trade. At least until the late 1960s, the predominant view was that export opportunities for developing countries were very limited outside of the traditional staples of primary commodities, the demand for which was growing only slowly. Hence it was concluded that avoiding import strangulation required a continuing effort to produce more and more industrial goods at home (the famous import substitution). But it became clear over time that developing countries are in fact perfectly capable of producing manufactured goods for the world market, if they start off realistically by producing goods intensive in resources and unskilled labor, and then work their way up gradually to more high-tech products as their industrial experience accumulates. This alternative strategy of export orientation has clearly proved more capable of overcoming the balance of payments constraint and supporting rapid growth. Today there is a very wide consensus in favor of export orientation.

Views in South Asia have moved in line with the change in the world consensus. Policies have changed in consequence, although in a relatively gradual way. This study provides perhaps the first attempt to take a comprehensive look at what the process of integrating South Asia into the world economy has already accomplished, at the potentialities for further integration (on a regional as well as a global basis), and at the implications for the region of the Uruguay Round, especially its provisions on clothing and textiles. The study considers also the implications of capital mobility, as the region is plugged into the world capital market and as it opens its doors to foreign direct investment.

The message of the report is essentially: so far, so good. Exports have responded to the new opportunities. The economies are opening up. Direct investment inflows are increasing. Relations within the region are improving. The Uruguay Round will offer important new opportunities. But the study also makes it clear that South Asia still has a long way to go. It still has the highest tariffs in the world; it still has more quantitative restrictions than most other regions; it is still less open than other regions; its intraregional trade is still miniscule; its inflow of direct investment is still modest compared to other regions. The study's conclusion is, nonetheless, optimistic. The analysis suggests that few regions have as much to gain from the worldwide trend toward increased integration as South Asia, and the prospects for the region fulfilling this potential seem favorable.

John Williamson
Chief Economist
South Asia Region
The World Bank

SUMMARY

South Asia has made much progress in deregulation and liberalization in the 1990s but still remains one of the least integrated regions of the world.

South Asia's average nominal protection rates are now around 20-25 percent, half what they were five years ago, though vast sectors, notably agriculture and consumer goods in India, have remained unaffected by liberalization. Real exports grew at 11 percent a year in the 1990s, faster than in any other region except East Asia. Nevertheless, per capita exports are five times lower than in other developing countries, and South Asia's share in world trade is just 1 percent, compared with 4 percent for China. Private capital flows to South Asia increased sharply in the 1990s. By 1996, however, its share of net private flows to developing countries was 4.3 percent, down on the 7.6 percent recorded in the 1980s. Foreign direct investment (FDI) was about 0.5 percent of the region's GNP in 1996, compared with 4.2 percent for East Asia and 1.9 percent for other developing regions. And, while FDI is stimulating growth of the export sector in countries such as China, in India it is still directed to protected domestic markets.

These broad trends mask wide disparities among South Asian countries. For example, despite much progress in trade liberalization in recent years and rapid export growth, India remains a relatively protected economy exhibiting low import penetration, even after account is taken of its size. At the other extreme, Sri Lanka and Nepal, are small and relatively open economies. Pakistan and Bangladesh stand somewhere in between. Over the last twenty years or so, no country in South Asia has achieved the speed of integration (measured by the change in the real trade ratio) of the average of all developing countries, and East Asia has exhibited speed of trade integration about three times that of South Asia. In the 1990s, India, Pakistan, and Sri Lanka have attracted some foreign direct investment, but, expressed as a share of GDP, none have attracted flows matching the developing country average. In the region, only India has succeeded in attracting significant amounts of portfolio flows.

For India, recent evidence suggests a strong response by private investment to economic reforms, as well as improved competition in domestic markets and a reduced role for the public sector in the economy. For other countries in the region, it is still unclear whether the change in economic incentives has been deep enough to produce long lasting effects on the industrial structure, inducing widespread economic restructuring and adjustment. Data show that, while the share of manufacturing in the region's total exports has increased from 50 percent in 1980 to about 75 percent in 1995, the share of manufacturing in output has risen only marginally, and the manufacturing sector has not absorbed the labor shed by agriculture.

Intraregional trade (often a sign of increased integration) remains tiny, but the prospects for increased regional cooperation are good.

Accounting for only 4 percent of total trade, intraregional trade is modest in South Asia, unlike the faster-integrating regions of East Asia, Latin America, and, more recently, Eastern Europe. In recent years, however, the region's leaders have been intensifying efforts toward furthering regional cooperation in the belief that it will reduce regional tensions and stimulate trade and investment. Latest agreements include the sharing of river waters between India, Bangladesh and Nepal, setting up a Preferential Trading Arrangement and a commitment to create a regional free trade area by the year 2000. This would be highly desirable. The economic gains would be significant, especially for the smaller countries. And the intensification of cooperation could result in coordinated trade and investment reforms that would make the region a more attractive location for multinational companies and foreign capital. It would also considerably reduce political and border tensions. There would be additional economic benefits from reduced military spending (which, for example, accounts for 37 percent of public expenditure in Pakistan) following settlement of regional disputes.

If the current program of reforms continues, export growth in South Asia in the next decade is expected to be solid and integration will mean sustained growth.

Looking toward the next decade, the global economic environment is expected to be favorable, characterized by high world output growth, moderate interest rates, low inflation and declining oil prices. And while the export slowdown of 1996 is largely due to cyclical, rather than structural factors, South Asia stands to gain significantly from increased liberalization of trade regimes across the world and from phasing out the Multi-Fiber Arrangement. Gains in textiles and garments are estimated to be large, outweighing losses from the elimination of quota rents, reflecting the fact that South Asian countries are among the lowest cost producers and the most severely constrained by quotas under the Multi-fibre Arrangement. And new export markets in which South Asia is becoming established (notably fish and seafood, gems and jewelry, machinery and equipment and software), are anticipated to continue growing rapidly.

South Asia remains vulnerable to external shocks. Contributing factors are the strong concentration of exports in cotton textiles and garments, heavy reliance on imported energy (particularly for India and Pakistan), high level of external indebtedness, and the high share of volatile portfolio flows in foreign financing. This vulnerability is compounded by risks from internal macroeconomic imbalances, particularly the size of fiscal deficits: they are larger on average than all other regions of the world, with the exception of Sub-Saharan Africa, and high relative to available domestic savings. South Asia also needs to adjust to a shift in the pattern of external finance from concessional funding to higher-cost private lending.

Over the next quarter century, South Asia will experience big changes in its economic structure. India is expected to become a significant force in world trade.

The next quarter century is likely to bring significant changes to the world division of labor and to the pattern of international specialization thanks to the effects of widespread trade liberalization, inclusion of China in the World Trade Organization, the abolition of the Multi-fibre Arrangement and the economic emergence of big developing countries. Model simulations suggest that these changes will bring important benefits to South Asia, particularly a strong increase in exports, which could increase at twice output growth. They also suggest a different specialization pattern for India, compared with the rest of South Asia. Thus, India's comparative advantages will shift from labor-intensive to more capital- and skills-intensive sectors, such as light and heavy manufactures and especially machinery and equipment. By 2020, these three sectors will account for roughly 64 percent of total exports (compared with 28 percent in 1992), while apparel and textile exports will be less than 13 percent, half what they were in 1992. The comparative advantages of the rest of South Asia will remain in labor-intensive products and textile and apparel will continue to account for about half of total exports. But these countries will also present a more diversified export structure, with an increasing share of light manufactures and primary agriculture products.

The future may well bring faster growth to South Asia. But the challenges, in terms of policies and governance, are great. The reforms must be broad based—that is, extend well beyond trade and investment liberalization—and keep pace with advances in other countries. Fast reformers attract the best foreign investors and become competitive in segments where skills, technology and economies of scale are important. In South Asia, the unexploited potential for integration and growth is probably greater than in any other region. The low cost of labor, availability (particularly in India) of skilled workers, familiarity with the English language and, in most countries, well-established legal and judicial systems, a free press, and vibrant and confident private sectors are factors which would place South Asia in a good position to attract foreign investors and achieve extraordinary international competitiveness.

CHAPTER 1

ECONOMIC INTEGRATION

South Asia is home to more than 20 percent of the world's population but accounts for only 1.5 percent of the world's GDP and about 1 percent of world trade. Until the late 1980s, the region was one of the least internationally integrated because of long-standing import substituting policies and trade and industrial restrictions. The 1990s, however, saw a significant change. In response to fiscal and external imbalances inherited from expansionary policies of the previous decade, all countries in the region embarked on programs of stabilization and structural reforms. Progress has been significant and South Asian economies are now more open than they have ever been. But liberalization of trade and deregulation of markets must be intensified for the benefits of integration to translate into higher growth.

Some important questions need to be answered. How much progress did South Asia make in the 1990s in opening up the trade regimes and integrating with the world economy? How did economic structures respond to advances in integration? And how did exports perform?

Available information suggests that South Asia's integration has increased dramatically from a low base in recent years. For example, up to the early 1990s, South Asia's protection (as measured by tariffs and non tariff barriers) were among the highest in the world. By 1997, average nominal protection rates have halved and are now around 20-25 percent, although important areas remain unaffected by liberalization (for example, consumer goods in India). But the ratio of merchandise exports to GDP (another indicator of integration) is still among the lowest in the world. Adjusted trade ratios suggest more integration—though they should be treated with caution because of the large statistical and data errors associated with adjustment techniques. Thus, despite the recent opening up, most South Asian countries remain among the least integrated in the world.

For most South Asian countries there is still little evidence that the change in economic incentives from liberalization has produced substantial changes in the industrial structure, nor has it induced widespread economic restructuring and adjustment. Data show that while the share of manufacturing in total exports has increased from 50 percent in 1980 to about 85 percent in 1995, the share of manufacturing in output has risen only marginally, and the manufacturing sector has not absorbed the labor force shed by the agricultural sector. In India, however, private investment has responded strongly to reforms. There have also been reduced distortions in domestic markets, improved competition and less public sector involvement in the economy.

Annual export growth in the 1990s (11.4 percent) was much higher than in the 1980s (5.5 percent), largely the result of increases in world demand, improved competitiveness and a relaxation in export controls. Export growth in the 1990s was also faster than that in any other developing region, with the exception of East Asia. But the starting point was so low that real per capita exports in South Asia are still the lowest of any industrial or developing region—about five times less than the average for low-and middle-income countries. Shares in the import markets of industrial countries have increased but they, too, remain small (around 1 percent), despite substantial redirection of South Asia's exports from markets in Eastern Europe and countries of the former Soviet Union to industrial countries and East Asia. Moreover, despite an important shift from primary to manufacturing goods, new exports are only a small share of the total.

I. SOUTH ASIA'S ECONOMIC PERFORMANCE IN INTERNATIONAL PERSPECTIVE

Compared with other developing regions (in particular East Asia), South Asia in the 1960s and 1970s had lower GNP per capita, poor social indicators and high dependency ratios that hampered any rapid rise in savings; yet, the region maintained macroeconomic stability and avoided runaway inflation. GDP growth accelerated in the 1980s, partly because of preliminary steps towards domestic and external liberalization; a declining population growth and a rise in savings; and adoption of expansionary fiscal policies that eventually gave rise to internal and external imbalances (table 1.1). Unlike other regions, South Asia did not suffer from adverse terms of trade (more pronounced in Latin America and Sub-Saharan Africa), or interruption in the supply of external finance during the debt crisis. The best-performing countries, particularly in East Asia, were those that stabilized their economies, reduced fiscal imbalances and reformed trade and incentive regimes in the 1970s and, therefore, benefited from acceleration in world trade after the mid-1980s.

Table 1.1 GDP growth
(percent)

	Real GDP Growth (%)				Growth of real GDP per capita			
	1965-80	1981-90	1991-95	1996	1965-80	1981-90	1991-95	1996
World	4.3	2.9	2.0	2.9	2.3	1.1	0.5	1.4
High income countries	4.0	2.9	1.9	2.5	3.1	2.2	1.2	1.9
Low-Middle-income countries	5.7	2.7	2.3	4.5	3.4	0.7	0.7	2.8
South Asia	3.3	5.8	4.4	6.5	0.9	3.4	2.5	4.6
East Asia	7.5	7.3	10.5	8.6	5.1	5.6	9.1	7.4
Europe and Central Asia	5.9	2.1	-5.5	-0.3	5.0	1.1	-5.8	-0.8
Middle East and North Africa	6.6	0.6	2.6	4.1	3.7	-2.5	-0.1	1.4
Latin America	5.7	1.2	3.1	3.5	3.1	-0.9	1.3	1.9
Sub-Saharan Africa	3.7	1.9	1.4	3.8	0.9	-1.0	-1.2	0.8

Source: IEC, World Bank

At the beginning of the 1990s, all countries in South Asia launched comprehensive reform programs. These included reducing the level and dispersion of tariffs and removing quantitative restrictions; improving regulations on domestic and foreign investments; reinforcing competition in domestic markets; liberalizing financial markets and relaxing exchange controls to achieve current-account convertibility; and curtailing the role of the state sector in the economy.

Table 1.2 Exports, investment and fiscal deficits

	Real exports(GNFS) growth (%)			Real Gross fixed Investment Growth (%)			Per capita real exports(GNFS) (1987 constant US $)			Fiscal deficit as percent of GDP		
	1981-90	1991-95	1996	1981-90	1991-95	1996	1980	1990	1996	1981-90	1991-95	1996
World	4.5	6.6	5.8	3.0	1.8	3.6	547	713	952	-3.3	-3.5	n.a.
High income countries	5.1	6.0	5.8	3.5	1.1	3.0	2204	3388	4620	-3.0	-3.3	-3.0
Low-Middle-income countries	2.2	8.9	5.9	1.5	4.2	6.0	158	161	238	-4.7	-4.4	-2.4
South Asia	5.5	11.4	6.4	6.6	5.8	9.7	20	27	44	-8.4	-7.7	-6.8
East Asia	8.6	16.8	6.1	8.9	12.7	9.6	48	94	202	-1.7	-0.5	-1.5
Europe and Central Asia	0.5	6.0	4.0	0.8	-6.7	-3.8	439	423	574	-4.0	-9.3	-3.4
Middle East and North Africa	-1.5	4.3	4.6	-2.4	2.1	4.5	743	469	516	-3.5	-5.9	n.a.
Latin America	4.3	9.8	9.2	-2.9	6.2	8.6	262	324	507	-6.5	-0.8	-2.2
Sub-Saharan Africa	0.3	1.2	3.4	-1.9	2.7	7.1	183	141	131	-5.3	-7.4	-8.6

Source: IEC, World Bank

The effects on growth have been positive. In the 1990s, GDP growth in South Asia was above that of low-and middle-income countries,[1] though less than in East Asia. In India, GDP grew at around 7 percent a year in 1994-96, driven by growth in exports and investments. Real export growth accelerated from 5.5 percent to 11.4 percent in the 1990s. South Asia, however, remains the region with the lowest share of exports to GDP (10 percent of GDP in 1994-95 compared with 18 percent in low- and middle-income countries and 25 percent in East Asia) and the lowest real per capita exports (see Table 1.2). And South Asia was less successful than the average low- and middle-income countries in reducing the fiscal deficit, which was 7.7 percent of GDP in 1991-95, just marginally below the 8.4 percent reached in 1981-90. This was comparable to ratios in Sub-Saharan Africa and Eastern Europe and much higher than the 1 percent achieved by East Asia. Significantly, the deficit resulted mostly from rising current expenditures, while the ratio of public investments to GDP declined by about 1-2 percentage points.

II. SOUTH ASIA AND THE GLOBAL ECONOMY

How much does South Asia participate in the world economy? And has the pace of integration—defined as participation in the international markets for goods, services, capital, and labor—quickened since the beginning of reforms in the early 1990s?[2]

Measures of integration

The ideal measure of integration is the closeness of domestic prices, wages (price of labor) and interest rates (price of capital) to world prices.[3] This is difficult to calculate, however, and indirect *policy* measures are often used instead (see Dollar 1992 and Easterly 1993). These include average tariffs and quantitative restrictions on imports (which indicate divergence between domestic and international prices of goods) and institutional factors, such as membership in the World Trade Organization (which suggests commitment toward openness). Creditworthiness ratings provide an

---

[1] In developing countries, growth was influenced by the recession in industrial countries, the continuing disappointing performance in Africa; and the collapse of the political and economic system in Eastern Europe and in the former Soviet Union.

[2] Integration of labor markets is not discussed. At a global level it is still very low, as labor markets are segmented because of immigration policies and other barriers.

[3] If a country is perfectly integrated into the world market, domestic and external prices would be the same. Thus, in theory it is possible for a country to be perfectly integrated in world markets without having much trade if its endowments reflected closely those in the rest of the world.

Economic integration

indicator of access to world capital markets which are closely correlated with the risk premium on international borrowing.

Box 1.1 Integration and growth

Benefits. Increased participation in the world economy has benefits. These include more efficient allocation of resources due to changing the production structure closer to one's comparative advantage, domestic competition as a spur to achieving international standards of efficiency, wider options for consumers, the ability to tap international capital markets for smoothing consumption in the face of short-term shocks (as well as to achieve higher long-term growth), and exposure to new ideas, technologies, and products. Using alternative measures, some studies show the benefits of integration. Both the level and pace of integration are important. For example, slow integration of some developed countries in recent years is simply due to the fact that they are already highly integrated. On the other hand, China has been integrating rapidly, starting from a position of near autarky; but its current level of integration is no higher than that of other big countries. The Global Economic Prospects report (World Bank, 1996) provides evidence that fast integrators among developing countries saw per capita GDP growth of almost 2 percent a year over the past decade, comparable to industrial countries. Easterly (1993) found that an increase in distortion of input prices relative to world prices of one standard deviation was associated with 1.2 percentage point lower per capita GDP growth over 1970-85. Another study (Borensztein, de Gregorio, and Lee, 1995) found that a one percentage point increase in the ratio of FDI to GDP in 1971-89 was associated with a 0.4-0.7 percent higher annual growth of per capita GDP. The impact was larger with higher educational attainment, a measure of a country's ability to absorb technology. Sachs and Warner (1995) examined a group of countries over 1970-89 and found that open economies within the developing countries group grew 4.5 percent and closed economies only 0.7 percent.[4]

Why do more open and integrated economies grow faster? There are several possible channels (Wacziarg (1997):

- Traditional trade theory stresses allocative efficiency: higher levels of output are attainable when countries specialize according to their comparative advantage.
- Factor accumulation and the investment rate: Trade liberalization may accelerate investment by allowing access to bigger markets. This permits greater exploitation of increasing returns to scale, thus providing the kind of 'big push' which has been argued to be necessary for developing countries to move from a low growth equilibrium to a sustained growth path.[5] It may also permit imports of previously unavailable or cheaper capital goods, removing constraints on investment.
- Knowledge spillovers are likely to be more prevalent in open economies, because of: knowledge that is embodied in traded goods and machinery and greater interaction or competition with sources of such technological innovation; and knowledge spillovers from foreign direct investment that is attracted to more open economies.
- Improved income distribution: returns to relatively abundant factors of production will tend to be higher in more open economies. In many developing countries, there is an abundance of unskilled labor. Empirically, greater openness is found to be associated with less income inequality. The latter, in turn, is found to be associated with more growth.

Government policy improvements are another possible source of faster growth in more open economies because of greater pressure on governments to maintain macroeconomic stability and a reduced role of government in the economy.

A recent cross-country empirical study attempts to measure the impact of more open trade policy on growth through these different transmission channels (Wacziarg 1997). The results suggest that the effect of more open trade through higher domestic investment may well be the most important, followed by government policy improvements. In the case of China, fast investment growth since 1978—conditioned by the increased openness of the economy—appears to have had a big effect on growth.

---

[4] On the relationship between integration and growth see also : D. Ben-David (1993), J.A.Frankel and D.Romer (1995).

[5] See, Kevin, Schleifer and Vishny (1989)

Integration can also be measured by quantity variables, such as ratios of trade to income, foreign direct investments to income, and the share of manufactures in a country's exports, an imperfect measure of a country's ability to conform to international standards and absorb technology. Quantity measures, however, are susceptible to a systematic influence such as size. For example, the trade to GDP ratio is inversely related to the size of the country.

The rest of this section reviews South Asia's trade integration with the world economy using both policy and quantitative measures: indicators of trade policy, trade to GDP ratios, and prices. Measures of financial integration are discussed in chapter 2. Not surprisingly, given that most South Asian economies (with the exception of Sri Lanka) were virtually closed until the late 1980s, all indicators suggest rapid progress in international integration although the level of integration today remains low compared with other countries.

Trade policy: 1996-97

Trade liberalization has been an important component of the structural reform program undertaken by South Asian countries. In the early 1990s, South Asian tariff and non-tariff rates were among the highest in the world (see table I.15, Annex I.1). Bangladesh had the largest unweighted average tariff rates for manufactures (85 percent), followed by Pakistan (64 percent), and India (56 percent); by contrast the figure for China was 40 percent, for Korea 11 percent, Indonesia 18 percent and Thailand 42 percent. India also had the highest ratio of imports covered by non-tariff measures (covering 72 percent of primary goods and 59 percent of manufactures).[6] While remaining high, trade protection in South Asia has declined significantly since the early 90s. The average unweighted tariff level for the region is now around 25 percent, half what it was in the early 1990s and non-tariff barriers remain significant only in India in the agriculture and consumer-goods sectors.

In *Bangladesh* the maximum tariff is currently 45 percent, down from 60 percent just two years ago. The unweighted average tariff rate is 21.8 percent and the import weighted rate is around 17 percent. The tariff structure is complex, however, comprising seven tariff rates. Most products can be freely imported with the exception of those in a controlled list, representing 2 percent of imports and covering roughly 25 percent of textile production. Exports of about 20 product categories are banned or restricted (to ensure supply to the domestic market). These include wheat, pulses, onion, jute, petroleum products, milk, shrimps and frozen fish. Incentives are given to exporters in the form of special bonded warehouses, export processing zones and duty drawbacks. Under the duty drawback scheme, direct and indirect exporters are exempt from import restrictions. Bonded warehouses allow exporting firms to import and stock duty-free inputs. There are two export processing zones (in Chittagong and Dhaka).

In *India*[7] for the current fiscal year, the 1997-98 Budget reduced the maximum tariff to 40 percent and the import-weighted average tariff to 20.3 percent (down from 22.4 percent in 1996-97 and 87 percent in 1990-91). It also eliminated licensing requirements for about a third of

---

[6] In India, before 1991, almost all imports were prohibited or licensed. Bulk items such as cereals, petroleum, metals, fertilizers etc. were canalized, that is they could be imported only by a Government monopoly. Since 1991 most imports of capital goods have been liberalized and substituted with tariffs but most consumer goods still remain under quantitative restrictions. In 1990-91 the unweighted average nominal tariff was 125 percent with a peak rate of 355 percent.

[7] See Pursell (1996).

consumer goods. It is estimated that quantitative restrictions, however, still cover about 44 percent of value added in manufacturing and 93 percent in agriculture. Exports of most manufactured products are free. Exceptions include those that are prohibited (for health or environmental reasons) or restricted (crude oil and petroleum products, fertilizers, cotton yarn and so on) or subject to minimum export prices. Exports of rice and other products (including fish, wheats, processed cereals, fruits) have been liberalized. Export incentives include: schemes to allow exporters to import inputs freely and, for some items, exempted duties; bonded warehouses; six export processing zones; a scheme to exempt exporters from profit taxes on exports; schemes to subsidize export credit and export credit insurance; and support and subsidies for export marketing.

In *Nepal* all goods can be freely imported with the exception of items such as arms, ammunition, wireless transmitters, precious metals and jewelry. Tariff rates are grouped into four bands. A few items are subject to a 110 percent rate (passenger vehicles, firearms, liquor and tobacco).

In *Pakistan,* the maximum tariff is now 45 percent, down from 65 percent in 1996 and 225 percent in 1988. The tariff regime, however, continues to have many exemptions and concessions, but these are being phased out. In 1995 the average rate of statutory duty was 58.2 percent while the import weighted average duty was 25.2 percent. Except for agricultural products, most goods can be freely imported. Exports are duty free, except for specified commodities (certain grains and dairy products, live animals, pulses and beans, timber). A few exports are subject to quotas (maize, gram, split gram and camels), quality controls or minimum export prices. Under the Export Processing Unit Scheme, selected industries with an export-output ratio of at least 50 percent (for example, textiles and clothing, leather, chemicals, electronics) can import raw materials, intermediate goods and capital goods free of import duties and local taxes.

In *Sri Lanka,* the maximum tariff is 35 percent (on consumer goods). On capital goods and raw materials the rate is 10 percent and on intermediate goods, 20 percent. Sri Lanka, however, has announced plans to switch to a 15 percent flat rate. No prior licensing is required for most imports with the exception of some agricultural products (potatoes, onions, chilies) and a few items that require a license for health or religious reasons. Other 'reserved items' (wheat, guns, explosive and some chemicals) are restricted to government or state corporations. Exports are free except for a few that require a license: coral and ivory products, timber, wood and passenger motor vehicles registered in Sri-Lanka. Quality control is exercised by State Boards over the exports of particular products (for example, gems).

Trade Openness

Countries that are highly integrated in the world economy tend to exhibit a high trade to GDP ratio, the so-called 'openness ratios'. In 1975-79, this ratio was 18 percent for South Asia, the lowest amongst all regions (table 1.3)[8]. By 1990-94, it had risen to 25 percent, but still remained the lowest in the world. The change (or pace of integration), was 0.5 percent per year, lower than the average for all developing countries (0.7 percent). By 1995, all countries had increased their

---

[8] Exports and imports of goods and non-factor services as a share of GDP measured at market exchange rates.

trade to GDP ratios, particularly India (26.4 percent), Bangladesh (36.7 percent), and Sri Lanka (78.6 percent). But so did other countries, especially China (45.7 percent).

Table 1.3 Trade to GDP ratios 1975-79 to 1990-94

Region or group	Nominal level 1975-79 %	Nominal level 1990-94 %	Annual average change (% Points)
World	34.7	39.2	0.3
OECD	34.2	35.4	0.1
USA	17.6	21.7	0.3
Japan	24.2	18.3	-0.4
Developing Countries	31.8	42.8	0.7
East Asia	31.2	54.6	1.6
China	10.0	35.8	1.7
Korea	63.8	58.2	-0.4
South Asia	17.6	25.1	0.5
India	14.1	21.0	0.5
Pakistan	30.7	36.4	0.4
Bangladesh	19.1	28.0	0.6
Sri Lanka	68.1	72.5	0.3
Nepal	25.4	42.1	1.1
Latin America	26.0	26.7	0.1
Brazil	16.3	15.6	0.0
Low-Income Countries	57.1	59.1	0.1
Large Developing Countries	25.6	36.2	0.7
Exporters of manufactures	74.7	88.5	0.9

Note: Trade = Exports and imports of goods and nonfactor services.
Source: World Bank

Price comparisons

Another measure of integration is the closeness of domestic to international prices of traded goods, expressed in a common currency. Trade barriers and other costs are a wedge between domestic and international prices and anecdotal evidence suggests these are still large in South Asia. Lack of empirical evidence, however, prevents a confirmation of this hypothesis.[9] A

---

[9] Two less recent studies, referring to the 1980s are worth noting : Easterly (1993) and Dollar (1992). Using Summers-Heston data on 1980 benchmark prices for 57 countries and 151 commodities, Easterly constructs a measure of price distortion which is defined as: the variance of the relative prices of inputs (in logs) across commodities for each country. According to this definition, prices in India are slightly more distorted than the average for all countries; but much more distorted in Pakistan and in Sri Lanka. Dollar also uses the Summers-Heston data base to compute price levels for 95 countries. He then constructs predicted price levels by adjusting actual values for characteristics such as GDP per capita and population density. The ratio of actual to predicted price level is taken as a measure of price distortion. Surprisingly, the Asian region shows price distortion levels that are lower than in developed countries! And within Asia, the South Asian countries fare better than the leading East Asian countries.

survey-based study of manufacturing units in Dehli indicated that while the intermediate inputs sector was highly protected this was not the case for cost of consumer goods.[10]

III. ECONOMIC STRUCTURE AND INTEGRATION

Did the economic structure in South Asia respond to the shift in economic incentives towards tradable goods engineered by the reforms in the early 1990s?

Historically, fast-integrating countries in Asia followed a path of development in which industry and manufacturing progressively increased their share of GDP at the expense of agriculture. Correspondingly, manufacturing and labor-intensive exports substituted traditional resource-based exports. As export-led growth led to rising labor costs, however, countries moved to more capital-intensive, technology, and service-based products. Thus, the service economy emerged through deindustrialization.

While agriculture has been the predominant sector, South Asia has been characterized by the early development of the service sector and not, as in East Asia, by industry and manufacturing (table I.16 in Annex I.I). For example, in the mid 1990s, industry contributed more than 40 percent of value added in East Asia, but only to a quarter in South Asia. In particular, manufacturing was only 10-20 percent of GDP in all South Asian countries compared, for example, with 38 percent in China, 29 percent in Korea, and 28 percent in Singapore and Thailand in 1993. Why these differences? First, the low outward orientation in South Asia and the lack of external markets hampered the emergence of economies of scale and confined the growth of the industrial sector to satisfy domestic demand. Second, regulation of the industrial sector (and an inflexible labor market) prevented faster growth and creation of employment opportunities in industry. At the same time, services, particularly in commerce, tourism and the informal sector, could absorb unskilled labor in agriculture and migration from rural to urban areas.

Structural changes in employment between 1965 and the late 1980s are mirror image of the output structure (table I.2, Annex I.I). Striking is the relative immobility, over a long period, in the occupational structure of the labor force. The agricultural sector continues, in the early 1990s, to be the main employer; but the labor force that moved out of agriculture was absorbed by the service sector while the share of the labor employed in industry declined in most countries. The services sector may have absorbed labor in personal services, trading, and tourism, and in the informal sector, including microenterprises that produce for exports, particularly in textile and clothing.

Export and import structure

Despite the painfully slow increase in the share of manufacturing in GDP, South Asian countries show a high share of manufactures in total exports (Figure 1.1). This is an imperfect, indicator of the extent to which countries are learning best practices and adopting new technologies. The ratio between manufacturing and total merchandise exports now varies between 76 percent in India to

---

[10] The policy implication was that consumer goods imports could easily be opened up with 50 percent custom duty. See National Council of Applied Research (1994).

93 percent in Nepal, an increase of around 20 percentage points since 1985 (table I.5, Annex I.I). South Asia's ratio of manufactures to merchandise exports grew fastest among all regions— 2.8 percent a year between 1980-84 and 1990-94, slightly ahead of East Asia.

In terms of final demand, exports of goods and services account for about 33 percent of GDP in Sri-Lanka, 16 percent in Pakistan, 14 percent in Bangladesh, and 12 percent in India. This is a different picture, for example, from the ultra export-dependent structure of smaller economies in East Asia—Singapore (169 percent), Hong Kong (143 percent), or Malaysia (47 percent).

The structure of merchandise imports reflects a process of late industrialization in most countries, in which the demand for capital and intermediate goods increased sharply in recent years (table I.3, Annex I.I). The share of consumer goods in total merchandise imports is insignificant in India (about 7 percent), as the market is highly protected by quantitative restrictions. By contrast, the openness of the trade regime in Bangladesh is reflected in a high share (43 percent) of consumer goods in total imports.

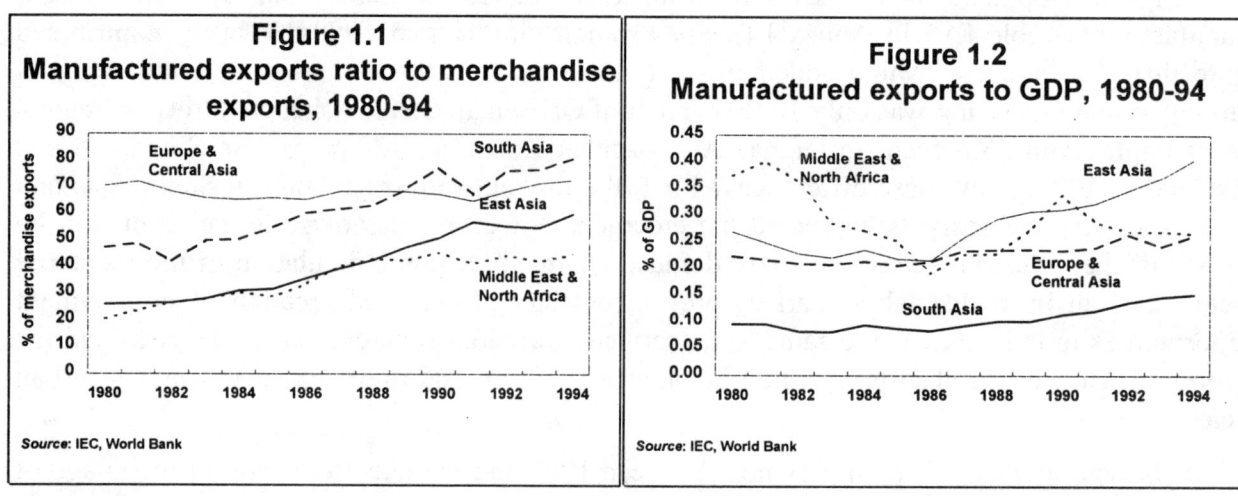

Figure 1.1
Manufactured exports ratio to merchandise exports, 1980-94

Source: IEC, World Bank

Figure 1.2
Manufactured exports to GDP, 1980-94

Source: IEC, World Bank

Product composition of exports

For South Asia, the product composition of exports has changed significantly in the past 10 years, shifting away from primary commodities (such as unprocessed cotton, jute and tea) to labor-intensive manufactures particularly garments and textiles, gems and jewelry and leather products. These eight sectors have increased their share of merchandise exports from 47 to 62 percent. So, although South Asia has diversified into manufactures its export structure has also become more concentrated. (figure 1.4). The most striking development has been in the garment sector where its share of merchandise exports has risen from about 5 percent in the early 1980s in India and Pakistan to 15 percent and 22 percent, respectively. In Sri Lanka and Bangladesh, the growth of garment exports has been even more dramatic rising from virtually zero to 46 percent of total exports in the former and 54 percent in the latter.

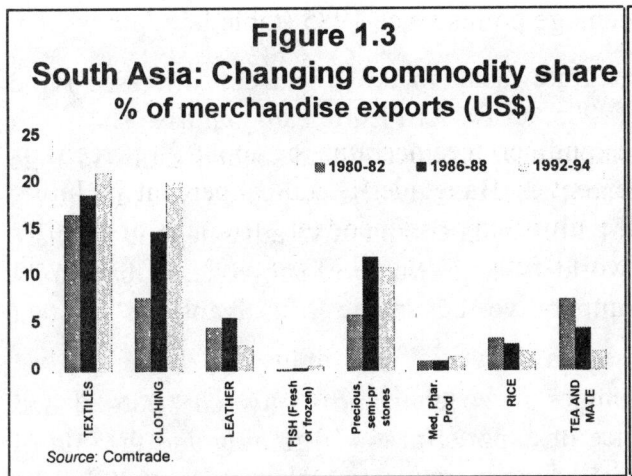

Figure 1.3
South Asia: Changing commodity share
% of merchandise exports (US$)

Source: Comtrade.

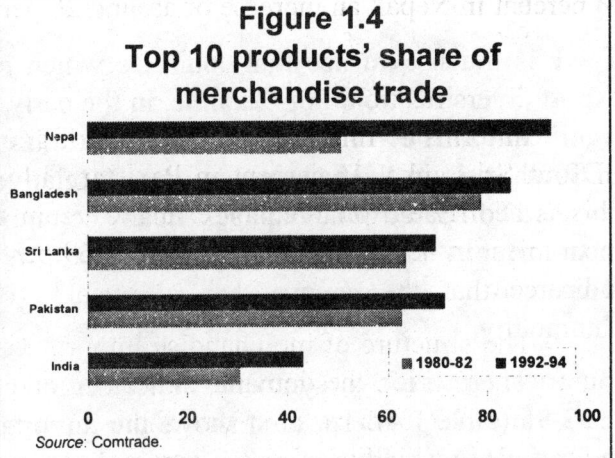

Figure 1.4
Top 10 products' share of merchandise trade

Source: Comtrade.

Growth of textile and clothing in South Asia

Textiles and clothing have played an important role in the industrialization of many countries, from the United Kingdom in the 18th and 19th centuries to the East Asian miracle economies in recent times (Anderson 1983, 1990). These labor intensive industries are a source of growth in employment and exports, and an initial step up the ladder of industrial development for many developing countries.

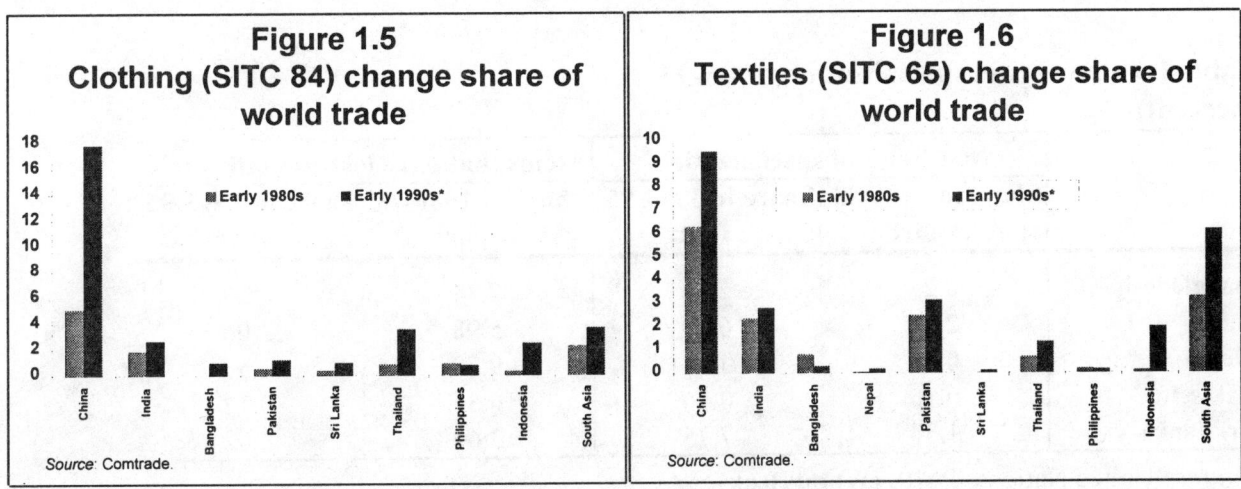

Figure 1.5
Clothing (SITC 84) change share of world trade

Source: Comtrade.

Figure 1.6
Textiles (SITC 65) change share of world trade

Source: Comtrade.

Competition in textiles[11] and clothing among developing countries has intensified over the past decade (Annex IV.I and figures 1.5 and 1.6). While South Asia's share of world exports of ready-made garments rose from 2.2 percent in the early 1980s to 3.6 percent a decade later, China's share soared from 5.1 percent to 17.8 percent. In textiles South Asia performed better, almost doubling its share to 6.2 percent. Within the region India and Pakistan are the only significant exporters, each accounting for roughly 3 percent of the world market.

---

[11] Throughout this report, textiles includes fibers, yarns, fabrics, and made-up items such as sheets and blankets. Apparel includes clothing, accessories, and headwear.

Specialization

There is much evidence that countries which integrate faster in the world economy see rapid export diversification. For example, in the early 1990s, all Eastern European countries showed a significant shift away from traditional specialization to new products.[12] Did specialization change in South Asia in the last decade or so? Relative specialization can be measured as a country's revealed comparative advantages. In any commodity, revealed comparative advantage is its share in the country's exports relative to its share in world trade. A value of more (less) than unity indicates that the country has a revealed comparative advantage (disadvantage) in that commodity.

There are two synthetic indicators of changes in specialization between 1986-88 and 1993-95 (table 1.4). The first shows the importance of exports (at the beginning and the end of the period) in which the country acquired new revealed comparative advantages. Conversely, the second indicator shows the importance of commodities in which the country was initially specialized but then had lost specialization. The results do not indicate any great movements in specialization. Noteworthy is the insignificance of 'new' items in which South Asian economies have become specialized: these represent 7.7 percent and 6.5 percent of exports in Sri Lanka and India, respectively (up from 1.5 percent and 2.3 percent). On the other hand, items in which South Asian countries were relatively specialized in 1986-88 (but where exports fell far enough for the revealed comparative advantage to become less than one in 1993 -95) accounted for 0.12 percent-3 percent of exports in the second period.

Table 1.4 Changes in specialization, 1986-95
(percent)

	New items of specialization[a]		Items that have lost specialization[b]	
	Share in 1986-88 export	Share in 1993-95 export	Share in 1986-88 export	Share in 1993-95 export
Bangladesh	0.27	2.81	2.34	0.29
India	2.35	6.50	5.98	3.06
Nepal	0.89	3.74	9.70	1.59
Pakistan	0.10	0.86	0.85	0.12
Sri Lanka	1.54	7.75	3.60	0.62

Source: United Nations, TARS (World Bank)

a/ Items where RCA86-88 < 1 and RCA93-95 > 1 (3-digit SITC)
b/ Items where RCA86-88 < 1 and RCA93-95 < 1 (3-digit SITC)

---

[12] See B. Hoekman, and S. Djankov (1996). They report calculations of changes in specialization for Easter European and FSU countries during the period 1988-1994. For example, in Bulgaria, items in which the relative comparative advantage was >1 in 1988 and <1 in 1994 accounted for 6 percent of total exports in 1994, down from 33 percent in 1988. Conversely, items in which it became newly specialized accounted for 26 percent of total trade in 1994, up from 5 percent in 1988. Items in which the Czech and Slovak Republics had been relatively specialized, but for which RCA had fallen below 1 in 1994 accounted for 19 percent of exports in 1994, down from 51 percent in 1988.

Level of technology

Another indication of how much countries are moving away from traditional products and into new high value-added exports is the share of technologically advanced goods[13] in manufacturing exports. This indicator provides a simple measure of whether an economy is advancing and producing goods of higher value added (figure 1.7).[14] East Asian economies have seen the fastest rise in the share of technologically advanced exports. South Asia is clearly the least advanced. In India, for example, these goods represented about 8 percent of

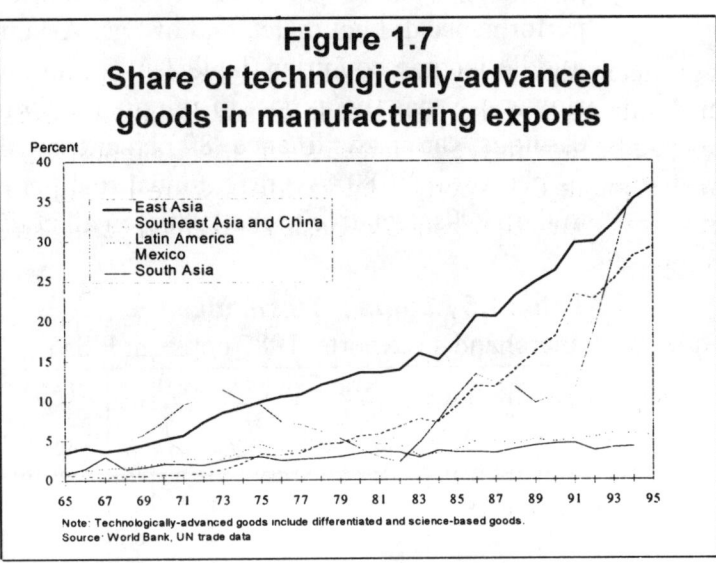

**Figure 1.7
Share of technolgically-advanced goods in manufacturing exports**

Note: Technologically-advanced goods include differentiated and science-based goods.
Source: World Bank, UN trade data

exports in 1994, just marginally up the 5.6 percent of 1975 (table I.6, Annex I). In China, the percentage of these exported goods increased from 8.8 percent in 1987 to 23 percent in 1995.

IV. EXPORT PERFORMANCE

For countries that are opening up, export growth is essential for balanced integration in the world market—that is, balanced and sustainable expansion in both imports and exports. Increasing export growth was one of the main objectives of the program of reforms undertaken by South Asian countries in the 1990s.[15] How did exports respond to these reforms?

Based on past performance (growth rates, market shares, competitiveness and redirection of exports) some things stand out:

---

[13] Technologically-advanced goods are defined as differentiated plus science-based goods. The classification is based on OECD (1987). Differentiated goods include: Engines and turbines (ISIC 3821), agricultural machinery and equipment (ISIC 3822), metal and woodworking machinery (ISIC 3823), special industrial machinery (ISIC3823, 3824), machinery and equipment (excluding electric not elsewhere classified) (ISIC 3829), electrical machinery, apparatus, appliances and supplies (ISIC 383), watches and clocks, photographic and optical goods (ISIC 3852/3). Science-based goods include: manufacture of other chemical products (which are mostly pharmaceuticals, and exclude industrial chemicals (classified scale-intensive)) (ISIC 352), office, computing and accounting machinery (ISIC 3825), aircraft (ISIC 3845), and professional, scientific, measuring and controlling equipment (ISIC 3851). (See Dasgupta and Imai , 1997). Exports are total merchandise exports, and include re-exports.

[14] East Asia includes China, Hong Kong, Indonesia, Korea, Malaysia, the Philippines, Singapore, Thailand. (The data on China becomes available only after 1987.) Taiwan (China) is not included. Southeast Asia include Indonesia, Malaysia, the Philippines, and Thailand. LAC include Argentina, Brazil, Chile, and Peru. South Asia include India, Pakistan and Sri Lanka. The figures for Mexico have been 3-year moving averaged (due to a large fluctuation).

[15] It included measures to remove obstacles to exports, the devaluation of the exchange rate and the elimination of quantitative restrictions on capital and intermediate goods.

- Compared with the 1980s, the 1990s has been a time of acceleration in real export growth rates for all the South Asian countries (see table 1.5). Although South Asia's performance did not match that of East Asia it was better than the average for low-and middle-income countries (table 1.2).[16] Moreover, growth of imports in the 1990s was slower, so that the export to import ratio improved markedly. For example, export earnings can now finance 80 percent of the import bill in India, against only 52 percent in 1980. Average annual real per capita export growth more than doubled in the 1990s, (relative to the 1980s) in all countries except Pakistan.

Table 1.5 Export performance
(merchandise exports, 1987 constant US$)

	Real Export Growth (%)			Per Capita Real Export (%)			Per Capita Real Export (US$)		
	1981-90	1991-95	1996	1981-90	1991-95	1996	1980	1990	1996
Bangladesh	6.6	17.6	10.1	4.0	15.7	8.1	8	12	28
India	5.7	12.0	8.2	3.5	10.0	6.3	14	20	34
Nepal	7.2	11.7	-2.2	4.5	8.9	-4.7	6	10	14
Pakistan	6.8	8.5	-1.5	3.5	5.4	-4.2	26	36	45
Sri Lanka	6.2	14.5	5.7	4.7	13.0	4.6	64	101	194

Source: IEC, World Bank

- Decomposition of export growth into quantity and price effects shows that in the 1990s more than in the 1980s, quantity effects have dominated (table I.8, Annex I.I). The performance of India and Bangladesh, driven by growth in volume, has been impressive. But the export performance of Nepal and Pakistan in 1991-95 was not as good as that of other South Asian countries.

- One feature of sustained integration is a well-diversified export base, geographically as well as by product. The 1990s saw a redirection of exports towards industrial countries, in particular the US and the European Union (EU) for Bangladesh, Nepal and Sri Lanka and towards East Asia for India and Pakistan away from Eastern Europe and republics of the former Soviet Union (see table I.9 in Annex I.I). The largest contribution to export growth in the 1990s came from the European market (53 percent for Bangladesh, 47 percent for Nepal, 47 percent for Sri Lanka and 26 percent for India), followed by the US market (contributing to 54 percent of the growth in Sri Lanka, 43 percent in Bangladesh, 37 percent in Nepal and 25 percent in India). The share of South Asian countries in the US and EU markets is still small—about 1 percent. East Asia is becoming increasingly important as an export market for India and Pakistan, but not for other South Asian countries. By contrast, East Asia is responsible for about 60 percent of import growth in all South Asian countries, up

---

[16] For example, average annual export volume growth during the period 1991-95 was 17 percent in China, about 13 percent in Indonesia, Korea, Myanmar and the Philippines, 18 percent in Thailand; 8.8 percent in Low and Middle Income countries, 9.7 percent in Latin America and the Caribbean's, 2.3 percent in the Middle East and North Africa, 1.1 percent in Sub-Saharan Africa.

from 27 percent in the 1980s. Meanwhile, imports from the US, the EU, and Japan are falling.

- The evolution of competitiveness as tracked by movements in the real exchange rate varies from country to country (Table 1.14, Annex I.I). Between 1990 and 1993, the real effective exchange rate depreciated by about 28 percent in India, then remained practically unchanged until 1996. In 1990-96 it depreciated by 20 percent in Bangladesh, less in Pakistan and Nepal but appreciated in Sri Lanka. The evolution of world demand, or market growth rate, was more favorable for India and Sri Lanka, reflecting the broader spectrum of exports.[17] The gain in market shares (approximated by the difference between changes in volume export growth and changes in the region's market growth.) shows a clear relationship between devaluation of the weighted real effective exchange rate, lagged two years, and changes in international demand (figure 1.8).

Figure 1.8
South Asia: Gain in export market volume and real effective exchange rate, 1989-1996

Depreciation of real effective exchange rate with two years' lag

Gain in export market volume

Note: Gain in Export Market = changes in real export growth minus changes in world demand
Source: IEC, World Bank, International Financial Statistics, IMF

The 1996 Slowdown

Comparisons between the recent export performance of South Asia, East Asia and the world, and other regions shows many similarities (figure 1.9). The acceleration (between mid-1994 and mid-1995) and subsequent slowdown in exports in 1996 for both South and East Asia reflects worldwide factors. First, when the dollar depreciated against the yen and major currencies in 1995, growth in world exports denominated in dollars accelerated simply as the result of the increase in dollar prices. Conversely, as the dollar strengthened in the later part of 1995 and 1996, dollar-denominated exports appeared to slow down. For example, the G-5 manufactured unit value index, expressed in US$, fell by 4.2 percent in 1996, having risen by 8 percent in 1995. Second, in volume terms, world export growth declined from 9.5 percent in 1994 to 8 percent in 1995 and to about 5.5 percent in 1996. Growth of South Asia's exports of goods and non factor services was 6.4 percent in

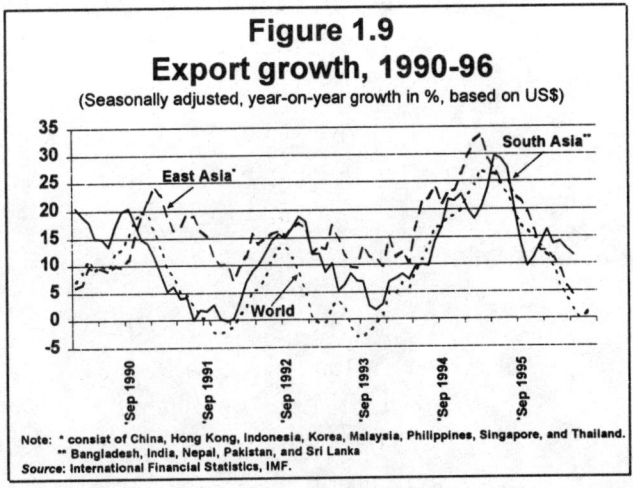

Figure 1.9
Export growth, 1990-96
(Seasonally adjusted, year-on-year growth in %, based on US$)

South Asia**

East Asia*

World

Note: * consist of China, Hong Kong, Indonesia, Korea, Malaysia, Philippines, Singapore, and Thailand.
** Bangladesh, India, Nepal, Pakistan, and Sri Lanka
Source: International Financial Statistics, IMF.

---

[17] For each country international demand is measured as a weighted average of the real imports of all trade partners, weighted by their share in total exports of each country.

volume terms in 1996, higher than that of the world (5.8 percent) and of most East Asian countries (for example, 4.6 percent in China). In South Asia, domestic factors have also played a part in the slowdown. The deterioration in competitiveness between 1993 and 1996 and the increase in the cost of finance, political instabilities in all countries but particularly Pakistan.

A conclusion of this chapter is that in the 1990s South Asia significantly improved its export performance. Exports were helped by favorable world trade conditions, exchange rate devaluation and the first effects of large-scale deregulation conditions that may not be there in the future. While the 1996 export slowdown is primarily due to cyclical factors, stabilisation of the real exchange rate may not be compatible with continued gains in market share.

CHAPTER 2

FINANCIAL INTEGRATION

Developing countries are becoming more integrated into international financial and capital market, as seen in the growth of private capital flows—3.7 percent of developing countries' fixed investment in 1990 to 14 percent in 1995, or more than double the rate before the debt crisis. Financial integration has been driven partly by investors' needs to diversify portfolios but mainly by the higher creditworthiness of developing countries, a result of deregulation of domestic financial and capital markets and improved macroeconomic fundamentals. So, how integrated is South Asia with international financial markets (in terms of foreign direct investment and equity and portfolio investment)? And to what extent has access to capital markets improved since reforms began in the early 1990s?

- In the 1990s, private capital flows to South Asia increased sharply. By 1996, they were running at five times the average of the 1980s. Cross-regional comparison, however, point to a declining share of resource flows. In 1996, South Asia's share of total net private flows to developing countries was 4.3 percent, compared with 7.6 percent in the 1980s.

- Net flows of foreign direct investment (FDI) to South Asia are now much higher than in the early 1990s but were only 0.5 percent of the region's GNP in 1996 ($2.6 billion) compared with 1.6 percent for Latin America, 0.8 percent for Sub-Saharan Africa, 4.2 percent for East Asia and 1.9 percent for all developing countries. By contrast, portfolio equity flows increased from zero to twice the size of FDI inflows by 1996. But India is practically the only country receiving substantial portfolio investment (about $5.4 billion in 1996 or roughly 12 percent of the developing-country total). New international equity issues have been uneven and unstable, and activities have slowed since 1995. Portfolio debt flows (international bond issues) remain limited, with the region's share accounting for less than 2 percent of the developing-country total.

- Since 1993, access to capital markets (as measured by the credit ratings of the Institutional Investor) has improved for all countries, except Pakistan. India has also succeeded in launching international bond issues on terms that were better than the average for developing countries.

- Increased financial integration of South Asia in recent years is partly the result of improved macroeconomic conditions and of the liberalization in investment regimes. Policy and incentives regimes, however, lack transparency and still involve government intervention. For example, the unusually large gap between approved and actual FDI flows (particularly in India and Bangladesh) may point to administrative inefficiency which delays implementation of projects.

- There is a striking difference between the pattern of FDI in South Asia and other regions. Inflows to South Asia are not being directed to export sectors, but are financing projects in the protected industrial and oil sectors. Thus, South Asia may be benefiting little from trends toward the globalization of production, as multinationals relocate various stages of assembly and marketing networks across countries. There are, however, some promising developments which may be due to recent liberalization policies—inflows of FDI in the services, following the opening up of regulatory regimes (the telecommunications and power sectors in India, for instance); and, also in India, FDI in all sectors has been associated with increasing technology transfers, helped by the automatic approval granted to technology agreements in priority areas.

I. FINANCIAL INTEGRATION: MEASURES, BENEFITS AND RISKS

Measures. Financial integration, that is, participation in international financial and capital markets) can be measured in various ways.[18] One is the country's access to international financial markets, based on country risk ratings (for example, by the *Institutional Investor's* Survey). Ratings also measure access to private capital markets: countries with higher ratings normally borrow more, for longer maturities and at lower rates than countries with low ratings. Financial integration can also be measured by a country's ability to attract private external financing, as reflected in the ratio of FDI and portfolios flows to GDP or the level of diversification of a country's financing (the more diversified, the deeper and more sustainable integration is likely to be).

Benefits. The benefits of financial integration stem from four main sources. First, financial integration can boost growth by raising domestic investment, which can be financed by foreign savings. Second, shifting the investment mix towards projects with a higher (risk-adjusted) rate of return, through knowledge and efficiency spillovers (especially from FDI). Third, by stimulating financial sector deepening, competition, and development. Fourth, financial integration allows individuals and firms to insure themselves against adverse developments in their home markets and smooth temporary declines in income.

Empirical evidence shows that FDI promotes economic growth in host countries (Blomström, Lipsey, and Zejan, 1992). This appears to be more significant than other types of external flows and than domestic investment (Husain and Jun, 1993; Borenzstein, De Gregorio, and Lee, 1994). The beneficial 'spillover' effects of FDI are due to several interrelated factors, including improvements in productivity, technology transfer, R&D expansion, and promotion of exports.

There are many benefits of portfolio flows (and, to a lesser extent, commercial bank flows) and from opening stock markets to foreign investors. These include wider access to international capital at lower cost, risk sharing and pricing, and greater efficiency in the allocation of capital. The cost of capital is likely to be lower because foreign portfolios can be diversified across national boundaries so reducing exposure to country-specific risk, resulting in lower risk premia.

---

[18] See World Bank (1997). In this chapter we are not discussing the extent to which asset prices are equalized across markets, which is another measure of financial integration: such a measure is more appropriate for industrial economies. In developing countries onshore and offshore yields (for the same instruments in the same currency) are likely to be different because of capital controls, transaction costs, political risks, etc.

Box 2.1 Evidence on economic benefits of FDI

Productivity. FDI can generate productivity gains through efficient production and management practices. Even where productivity improvements from FDI come at the expense of local entrepreneurs, FDI tends to bring in 'net' productivity gains to the host country (Lipsey, 1996). There are plenty of country-specific examples to demonstrate the benefit of such productivity gains. In Mexico, for example, the higher the degree of foreign ownership, the faster the growth in labor productivity and the faster the rate of catch-up by Mexican-owned firms. In Hungary and Czech Republic, too, productivity growth of foreign affiliates far outpaced that of domestic firms (UNCTAD, 1995). In Morocco, sectors with a high presence of foreign-controlled firms tend to have lower variance of productivity. Recent Japanese MITI surveys also provide evidence of productivity gains from Japanese FDI projects, especially in Asia.

    Technology transfer and R&D expansion. FDI can promote technological changes in developing countries directly through its contribution to higher factor productivity, changes in product and export composition, R&D management practices, and employment and training. Indirect benefits come through collaboration with local R&D institutions, technology transfer to local downstream and upstream producers—so-called 'vertical' spillovers.

    The first quantitative evidence of positive spillovers was from direct investment in manufacturing by U.S. firms (Dunning, 1958). Recently, a positive spillover on growth from technology transfer was found for a sample of 69 developing countries (Borenzstein, De Gregorio, and Lee, 1994). This confirmed similar conclusions of earlier studies (for example, Blomström, Lipsey, and Zejan, 1992). Productivity tends to be higher in developing countries having strong trade links with OECD countries, possibly reflecting the close trade-FDI relationship and its contribution to technology upgrading. FDI in China proved to be the source of technology transfer—on evidence drawn from the relative performance of foreign-invested firms, compared with local enterprises, in rural areas (Wei, 1996).

    An influence on host-country economies often neglected is R&D by multi-national corporations in developing countries. Some foreign affiliates (especially U.S.) account for significant shares of total R&D in some developing countries, including Brazil and Mexico. Cross-border R&D has grown substantially in recent years: in the U.S., 15.4 percent of all R&D in industry was conducted by foreign affiliates in 1990, compared to 6.4 percent in 1980, and the share of multi-national affiliates in national R&D spending exceeded 15 percent in a number of countries, including Korea and Singapore (Dunning, 1994).

    Export orientation. As part of their multicountry production and marketing strategies, multinationals increasingly export from host countries. The export propensity of U.S. FDI steadily grew through the mid-1970s: in 1977, foreign affiliates in developing countries exported about 18 percent of output, a threefold increase in two decades. The ratio of exports to output by U.S. affiliates more than doubled to 39 percent by 1993, from a low point at the onset of debt crisis, as U.S. affiliates in countries such as Brazil, Chile, and Mexico switched the geographical composition of sales from host-country markets to export markets (Lipsey, 1996).

    Export orientation of Japanese affiliates has also been growing, most notably in East Asia, where their exports accounted for 34 percent of total output in 1993. This is almost four times the export ratio of Japanese affiliates in North America. The growth in exports by Japanese affiliates in developing countries has been led by steadily rising home-bound exports, while exports to third countries account for a much smaller share and actually declined in the past decade. For instance, Japanese affiliates in China exported 53 percent of production in 1992, compared to less than 10 percent in 1986.

Risks. As the liquidity crisis in Mexico showed, large flows of portfolio investment to emerging capital markets—especially in local debt instruments—entail substantial risks, creating vulnerability in the domestic financial system and instability in economic management. Swings in portfolio flows make more difficult management of foreign reserves and monetary and exchange-rate policies.

    There are three separate elements of risk. First, surges in inflows of capital in the early stages of financial integration may be large relative to the size of the local economy, and difficult to manage if financial and capital markets are small and inflexible; for example, the cumulative capital inflows were 45-46 percent of GDP during the surge period in Malaysia (1990-94), Thailand (1988-1994), and Costa Rica (1987-1994). Capital flows to South Asia have, so far, been smaller. India's first wave of inflows were in 1992-94 and cumulatively amounted to 5.6 percent of 1994 GDP. The comparable figure for Pakistan was 6.3 percent in 1992-93.

Second, there may be a susceptibility to large reversals as recently experienced by Mexico. Other countries have also seen massive outflows, mostly triggered by a lack of investor confidence in domestic macroeconomic policies and a deterioration in sociopolitical conditions. Pakistan saw such a reversal in 1994-95, amounting to 4 percent of GDP, almost comparable to Mexico's 5 percent in 1994-95.

Third, the volatility associated with private capital flows makes countries more exposed to shocks in the international economy, such as changes in interest rates and stock market returns and can amplify the effects of domestic shocks. This is because emerging markets suffer from incomplete and asymmetric information, and weak institutional frameworks. Thus, domestic investors may be influenced by foreign investors, leading to even greater volatility.

II. TRENDS IN SOUTH ASIA'S FINANCIAL INTEGRATION

South Asia's financial integration with the international economy has increased in the past decade. Aggregate private capital flows were US$10.7 billion in 1996, four times the average in the 1980s (table 2.1). This was roughly equal to the inflow to Sub-Saharan Africa and ten times less than to East Asia. Not only is the absolute level of resource flows low in South Asia: its share in aggregate capital flows to developing countries has fallen from 7.6 percent in the 1980s to 4 percent in 1995-96, while flows to East Asia have almost doubled. Moreover, these flows are volatile. The bulk of recent increases has been in portfolio equity investment, which is more sensitive to the political and economic environment (table 2.2).

Table 2.1 Aggregate private capital flows (long-term) to developing regions, 1980-1996

(US$ billions)	Average 1980-89	1990	1991	1992	1993	1994	1995	1996
All developing countries	40.4	44.4	56.9	90.6	157.1	161.3	184.2	243.8
South Asia	2.7	2.2	1.9	2.9	6.0	8.5	5.2	10.7
Sub-Saharan Africa	2.6	0.2	0.8	-0.3	-0.5	5.2	9.1	11.8
East Asia & Pacific	9.1	19.3	20.8	36.9	62.4	71.0	84.1	108.7
Europe & Central Asia	6.8	9.5	7.9	21.8	25.6	17.2	30.1	31.2
Latin America & the Caribbean	15.3	12.5	22.9	28.7	59.8	53.6	54.3	74.4
Middle East & North Africa	3.9	0.6	2.2	0.5	3.9	5.8	1.4	6.9
(percent of total private capital flows to developing countries)								
South Asia	7.6	4.8	3.4	3.2	3.8	5.2	2.8	4.4
Sub-Saharan Africa	5.4	0.6	1.5	-0.4	-0.3	3.2	5.0	4.8
East Asia & Pacific	24.2	43.5	36.6	40.7	39.7	44.0	45.7	44.6
Europe & Central Asia	17.5	21.4	13.9	24.0	16.3	10.7	16.3	12.8
Latin America & the Caribbean	33.6	28.1	40.3	31.6	38.1	33.2	29.5	30.5
Middle East & North Africa	11.4	1.4	3.9	0.6	2.5	3.6	0.8	2.8

Note: 1996 data are estimates.

Source: World Bank, Debtor Reporting System.

Table 2.2 Private capital flows to South Asia
(US$ billions)

	1990	1991	1992	1993	1994	1995	1996
South Asia	2.2	1.9	2.9	6.0	8.5	6.0	13.4
of which:							
- FDI	0.5	0.5	0.6	0.8	1.2	2.0	3.4
- Portfolio capital	0.1	0.0	0.4	2.0	6.2	2.3	6.4
> International issues	0.0	0.0	0.246	0.34	4.27	0.28	1.50
> Local equity investment	0.1	0.0	0.135	1.68	1.95	2.05	4.90
- Other private	1.6	1.4	1.9	3.2	1.1	1.7	3.6

Source: World Bank, Debtor Reporting System

Foreign direct investment is increasing—but slowly

The level and pace at which FDI increases are important indicators of financial integration. FDI represented 0.1 percent of GDP in the late 1970s, compared to 0.8 percent in all developing countries. (table II.1 in Annex II.1). Since then it has been growing at 0.02 percent of regional GDP a year, much slower than in East Asia but about equal to the developing country average. Yet, in the early 1990s the ratio of FDI to GDP in South Asia was half that of all developing countries and less than a fifth that of East Asia. Consistent with a reduction in investment barriers and liberalization of economies, FDI shows a steady growth in more recent years reaching $2.6 billion in 1996. (Annex II.II, and table 2.3). But the aggregate size is still modest and FDI in South Asia accounts for less than 3 percent of FDI to all developing countries. South Asia also has the lowest ratio of FDI inflows to GNP (table II.6, Annex II.I). The share of FDI in South Asia's gross domestic investment remains low at less than 1 percent (compared with 1.6 percent for Sub-Sahara Africa and Latin America and 3.3 percent for East Asia).

Table 2.3 Foreign direct investment to developing regions, 1990—1996

	1990	1991	1992	1993	1994	1995	1996
(US$ billions)							
All Developing Countries	24.5	33.5	43.6	67.2	83.7	95.5	109.5
Sub-Saharan Africa	0.9	1.6	0.8	1.6	3.1	2.2	2.6
East Asia and Pacific	10.2	12.7	20.9	38.1	44.1	51.8	61.1
Europe and Central Asia	2.1	4.4	6.3	8.4	8.1	17.2	15.0
Latin America and Caribbean	8.1	12.5	12.7	14.1	24.2	22.9	25.9
Middle East & North Africa	2.8	1.8	2.2	4.2	3.0	-0.3	2.2
(US$ millions)							
South Asia	464.0	456.0	624.0	841.0	1231.0	1791.0	2632.0
Afghanistan	0.0	0.0	0.0	0.0	0.0	0.0	0.0
Bangladesh	3.0	1.0	4.0	14.0	11.0	2.0	15.0
Bhutan	0.0	0.0	0.0	0.0	0.0	0.0	0.0
India	162.0	141.0	151.0	273.0	620.0	1,300.0	2,300.0
Maldives	6.0	7.0	7.0	7.0	8.0	9.0	10.0
Nepal	6.0	2.0	4.0	6.0	7.0	8.0	7.0
Pakistan	244.0	257.0	335.0	346.0	419.0	409.0	200.0
Sri Lanka	43.0	48.0	123.0	195.0	166.0	63.0	100.0

Note: 1995 data are preliminary and 1996 data are estimates.

Source: World Bank, Debtor Reporting System.

The disparity between China and India is especially striking. Before 1979, FDI was virtually non-existent in both countries. By 1995, it represented about 6 percent of GDP and 25 percent of domestic investment in China and only 0.5 percent of GDP and 0.9 percent of domestic investment in India. China embarked on aggressive reforms about twelve years earlier than India and it took five years to pass the US$1 billion mark in FDI inflows, following liberalization of foreign investment laws and the setting up special economic zones in 1979. India's FDI buildup took, a similar path: FDI inflows exceeded the US$1 billion mark for the first time in 1995, four years after reforms were launched. FDI inflows in China have been spurred by liberalization and by high economic growth. Ninety percent of FDI has been directed to the coastal provinces, a result of government policies to attract foreign investors in special economic zones. China also benefited from the proximity to economically dynamic neighbors, such as Hong Kong and Taiwan, which India does not have.[19] Moreover, China benefited from a large overseas Chinese community responsible for the largest share of FDI.

FDI in India has come mostly from the US, directed to the consumer sectors (still protected by high tariff barriers,) and natural resource sectors (box 2.2). There is evidence that this has increased domestic competition and led to partnerships or mergers between Indian and foreign firms. But little has gone to export-oriented sectors, despite India's wage advantage. Inflexible labor legislation, low levels of literacy and poor service in transport, ports, power and communications, reduce the competitiveness of exports and the attractiveness of the country to multinational enterprises. By contrast, Bangladesh has been fairly successful in attracting FDI in its export processing zones, particularly in the ready-made garment sector, exploiting quota

---

[19] See N.K. Sengupta, A. Banik, and R. Kathuria, (1996).

restrictions imposed under the Multi-Fiber Arrangement. Political instability and civil unrest are almost certainly the main reason for low levels of FDI in Pakistan and Sri Lanka.

Box 2.2 Foreign direct investments in South Asian countries

India

    Overall trends. South Asia's FDI inflows, (and approved FDI) have grown substantially since the early 1980s[20]. Actual flows of foreign equity investment in 1995 were almost $2 billion, about thirty-five times higher than in the 1980s. The actual flows as percentage of approved investment remain low, however, at an average of 18 percent, which is about half the rate seen in many developing countries (including China) actively seeking FDI.

    Sectoral patterns. The distribution of FDI inflows by sector has changed much in recent years. The relative importance of manufacturing, while still the single most significant destination for FDI, has declined from 85 percent of flows in 1990 to 59 percent by 1995, following the opening up of infrastructure and services to direct foreign investment. Within manufacturing, FDI flows appears to have shifted from heavy capital goods to other industries. The top four—fuel (with a 28 percent share), chemical, services, and metals—account for more than 50 percent of all FDI approved since 1991. Textiles, an important source of exports, has attracted less than 4 percent of the total. FDI flows to India tend to focus on industries targeted at domestic markets, whereas China has been attracting FDI in export-oriented industries through special economic zones. Preliminary data for 1996 suggest that FDI in service sectors in India is growing fast. The share of FDI in telecommunications jumped to 24 percent of the total in 1996, thanks to approved foreign investment in cellular mobile telephones.

    Investment sources. The United States continues to be the leading source of FDI to India, accounting for 30.3 percent of the total approved in the post-liberalization period (through 1995), up from 25.5 percent in the 1980s. Other major sources are the United Kingdom (7.5 percent), Japan (5 percent), Switzerland (4.6 percent), and Germany (3.2 percent). In recent years the share of FDI from East Asia has also jumped. According to preliminary 1996 data, Korea was the leading source of FDI in India in 1996, second only to the United States. FDI flows to India fall into three classifications. There are those requiring prior Government clearance by the Foreign Investment Promotion Board or the Secretariat of Industrial Approval; those receiving automatic approval of the Reserve Bank of India; and non-resident Indian direct investment approved by the Reserve Bank. The share of non-resident Indian investments has declined substantially since 1991, possibly indicating that liberalization has helped to further diversify FDI sources. The largest share of FDI falls under the category needing clearance by the Foreign Investment Promotion Board and the Secretariat of industrial approval, which may reflect the large-scale investment projects in a few sectors, such as power and hydrocarbons.

Pakistan

    Overall trends. Recent FDI inflows to Pakistan have followed a gentle upward trend, with an average $100 million or so a year in much of the 1980s to more than $300 million in the first half of 1990s. Growth of FDI inflows (as well as the size), however, has been less impressive than in India, possibly because of political uncertainties and weak economic fundamentals.

    Sectoral patterns. Foreign investors interest in sectors producing for export markets has been limited, with the exception of textiles and agribusiness. For example, approved projects in the Karachi Export Processing Zone have totaled less than $100 million since its inception in early 1980s. More recently, an increasing amount of foreign investment has gone to service sectors, including privatization programs (for example, banks) and infrastructure. At end-1993, manufacturing accounted for about 60 percent of the total $650 million. The rest went to service sectors, with little going to agriculture and mining.

    Source countries. Roughly half of total FDI flows since the mid-1980s came from the US, mostly for oil exploration. In 1995, however, the US share of FDI inflows to Pakistan declined to less than a third, while FDI from Japan and Asian NIEs (notably, Hong Kong) has significantly increased. By contrast, the UK, once the dominant FDI investor in the country, has been disinvesting in recent years.

---

[20] See tables II.13-15 in Annex II.I.

Bangladesh

    Overall trends. No reliable data on FDI are currently available. The most reliable source is UNCTAD. According to the UN, FDI in Bangladesh reached $125 million in 1995, growing from an average of less than $10 million in the previous five years. The FDI approval data from the Board of Investment indicates a rising trend, about six times higher than the actual FDI flows—amounting to $720 million equivalent in 1995.

    Sectoral patterns. The two export processing zones (in Chittagong and Dhaka) have been the main channel for FDI inflows in manufacturing. Since its 1981 inception, 106 projects have been approved (by October 1995) in the Chittagong Zone Korea is the leading source of FDI in export processing zones, with a cumulative total of $56 million in 22 projects, followed by Japan ($46 million in 17 projects), Hong Kong ($16 million) and the United States ($11 million). The Dhaka zone has been in operation since 1993, and has approved $110 million for 36 projects. Korea also headed the FDI source countries in Dhaka, with $42 million, followed by Hong Kong ($27 million) and the United States ($17 million). Among the major sectors attracting FDI in EPZs, textile (including knit and leather) account for the bulk of foreign investment, followed by electric and electronic parts and metal products. Recent increases in FDI inflows went mainly to service sectors, notably, telecommunication.

    Source countries. FDI in Bangladesh originates mostly from Asia. In 1994-95, India, Japan, Korea, Malaysia, and Singapore were the leading sources, accounting for more than 70 percent of the total. The United States and the United Kingdom were the only significant non-Asian direct investors.

Sri Lanka

    Overall trends. FDI in Sri Lanka has grown steadily from less than $50 million a year in the late 1980s to an annual average of more than $130 million since 1993. Data on approved FDI, however, show a decline from $195 million in 1993 to $63 million in 1995 (a 43 percent fall on 1994 and the lowest since 1992), but a rise to $100 million in 1996. The recent downward trend may be attributed to the unsettled political and social situation and to revisions in the FDI incentive system (including the abolition of tax holidays in April 1994), although the new measures introduced in November 1995 reinstated a wide range of preferential treatment for FDI.

    Sectoral patterns. Roughly 55 percent of FDI flows since 1993 have gone to manufacturing sectors, slightly lower than their 60 percent share in cumulative FDI for 1978-93. Within manufacturing, the share of textile (clothing and leather goods) has steadily declined, although it remains the single largest sector attracting FDI, accounting for about 30 percent of all inflows. In contrast, agricultural products and beverage sectors and non-metal mineral products have taken an increasing share.

    Source countries. Based on approval figures (for end 1995), Singapore led the FDI source economies, with $240 million for 53 projects, including some big projects in telecommunications. Korea was the second leading investor with $184 million for 112 projects, mostly in light manufacturing, followed by Japan with $160 million for 81 projects, predominantly in clothing, electronic parts, and housing development. This was followed by Hong Kong ($93 million for 58 projects) and the United States ($90 million for 44 projects).

Portfolio flows

In the past 20 years, portfolio flows were concentrated mainly in high-income countries, the exception being Latin America.[21] Portfolio flows to developing countries grew rapidly from the late 1980s but remained concentrated in a handful of countries, mainly in East Asia. In only 17 of 70 developing countries sampled did portfolio flows exceed 0.05 percent of GDP in 1990-94. Most were East Asian, Latin American and Eastern European. Many of the remaining countries including those in South Asia, did not even average 0.1 percent of GDP.

---

[21] Portfolio flows are defined as investment assets (corporate securities, bonds, notes and financial derivatives) other than those included in FDI, and excluding exceptional financing and reserve assets).

Foreign investor participation in local stock markets soared in recent years (table 2.2). This was due to liberalization policies implemented by South Asian countries since the early 1990s and a trend toward greater diversification of institutional portfolios.

India alone attracted $4.6 billion of net portfolio equity investment in 1996. Investor interests appears to reflect the maturing stock market (with capitalization of $130 billion), secondary market liquidity and a growing number of listed stocks, helping to overcome the lack of transparency that had discouraged foreign interest in the previous years.

The rapid increase in portfolio equity flows to India is due to a number of factors. First, there are well-known corporate names with established track records on a liquid exchange. Second, structural reforms (including the elimination of licensing restrictions) initiated in 1991 enhanced the growth prospects for the Indian corporate sector. Third, restrictions on foreign portfolio investment were eased (particularly with respect to ownership limits). Fourth, the capital surge coincided with a tightening of monetary policy, partly because of high budget deficits which kept the domestic cost of borrowing high relative to the cost of funds raised abroad.

In *Pakistan*, portfolio investment steadily increased, from less than $100 million in 1991 to a peak of $1.3 billion in 1994, a result of the liberalization policies pursued in the 1990s and the opening of the power sector. But it plunged in 1996, reflecting worsening economic conditions and political instability.

Portfolio investment in *Bangladesh* remains negligible—about $40 million a year since 1994. However, with confidence growing in the new government and measures in the 1996-97 budget to encourage foreign investments, Bangladesh's stock markets recorded a spectacular bull run in the second half of 1996. [22] Market capitalization soared from $1.5 billion (4.3 percent of GDP) to $6 billion (17 percent of GDP) between June and mid-November 1996 and the share price index tripled. This was followed by a near crash, with the stock-market index diving by 50 percent between mid-November and late February 1997. Such stock market gyrations, however, do not appear to have been triggered by high turnover in foreign portfolio investment, judging from the relatively small foreign participation in local markets.

Sri Lanka attracted more than $100 million of portfolio equity investment in local stock markets in 1994, but since then sluggish market performance resulted in lack of foreign investor interest, with less than $70 million of annual portfolio investment.

Portfolio equity flows through international listings. South Asian countries have also benefited from international equity issues in the form of American Depository Receipts and Global Depository Receipts (table II.7 in Annex II.I). India has been the dominant player, with total issues more than $5 billion. Pakistan managed to issue international equities for $1.1 billion in 1994, at a time when international institutional investors made a large stock adjustment to their portfolio to include emerging-market instruments.

---

[22] Measures included exempting capital gains on bonus shares from the income tax, removing the lock-in requirement, introduced a year earlier, for foreign investments in Initial Public Offers and reserving 5 percent of primary issues for nonresident Bangladeshis.

International bond issues. Portfolio debt flows too have been largely confined to India and Pakistan, the two South Asian countries that have formal ratings from major international rating agencies (see table II.8 in Annex II.I). India has an investment grade of Baa given by Moody's, and its Standard & Poor's (B+) rating compares well against many other developing country-borrowers. Pakistan's rating has suffered from the recent economic weakness and political turmoil and remains at below-investment grade (according to ratings by both Moody's and S&P).

Prospects for more bond issues appear promising, especially for strong private sector borrowers. In January 1997, Reliance Industries, the Indian petrochemicals and textile group became the first private-sector company in Asia to make a so-called 'century' bond—that is a bond with a 100 year maturity, and successfully raised $100 million at 355 basis points above the U.S. Treasury bill rate. This company received the same rating as the sovereign rating for India.

Impact of capital flows on the domestic economy

What has been the impact of FDI and portfolio flows on South Asia? No comprehensive research is available. For India, however, two questions can be posed and answered. Has FDI in India been sufficiently export-oriented and has it contributed to the improvement in export performance? Also, did FDI contribute to technology transfers?

A recent empirical study reports no compelling evidence to support the positive role of FDI inflows in export promotion, which is largely consistent with the result of Kathuria (1996). This is hardly surprising since, as discussed earlier, a majority of FDI directed to India has been a domestic-market seeking type.

Recent liberalization of foreign investment in India has provided a stimulus for technology transfers by granting automatic approval of technology agreements in priority areas and freedom to hire foreign technicians. Some distinctive patterns before and after the liberalization are becoming evident (Subrahmanian, et al, 1996; Kathuria, 1996). First, an increasing proportion of technology transfer has taken place with foreign equity investment (as opposed to lump-sum payments such as for royalty and licensing) in almost all industries. Second, the number of agreements of 10 years and longer has been more than three times higher in the 1990s, indicating the potential benefit of local industry's access to advanced technology on a longer-term and continuous basis. Third, foreign affiliates tend to exhibit higher levels of multi-factor productivity, even after controlling for size differences.

The impact of foreign portfolio investment on India's capital market performance appears to have been largely positive, consistent with the experience in most emerging markets undergoing liberalization. Regression analysis confirms the significant positive correlation between the size of foreign investment and the rate of return based on monthly observations from January 1993 to December 1996. Regression estimates indicate that $100 million of foreign investment a month on average raised the local stock market return by roughly 3 percent.[23]

---

[23] Among the various model specifications, the most robust result was obtained from a simple contemporaneous regression for the monthly rate of return (RI) with the monthly net portfolio investment (PI) as the independent variable, namely: RI_t = intercept + PI_t. The parameter estimates show that RI_t = -3.74 (-2.38) + 0.03 (3.49), in the parentheses are t-statistics, which are significant at 1 percent level. R-square = 0.22

Market creditworthiness

Credit ratings by agencies are an important indication of a country's access to international capital markets and a determinant of the cost of funds. Countries with good ratings are generally able to borrow at lower rates and have access to diversified sources of funds. Credit ratings compiled by the Institutional Investor suggest an improved market creditworthiness in South Asia, with most countries experiencing an upturn since early 1990s (figure 2.1 and table II.10, Annex II.I). Among developing countries, India is well placed, rating 17th among 93 countries in 1993-95.

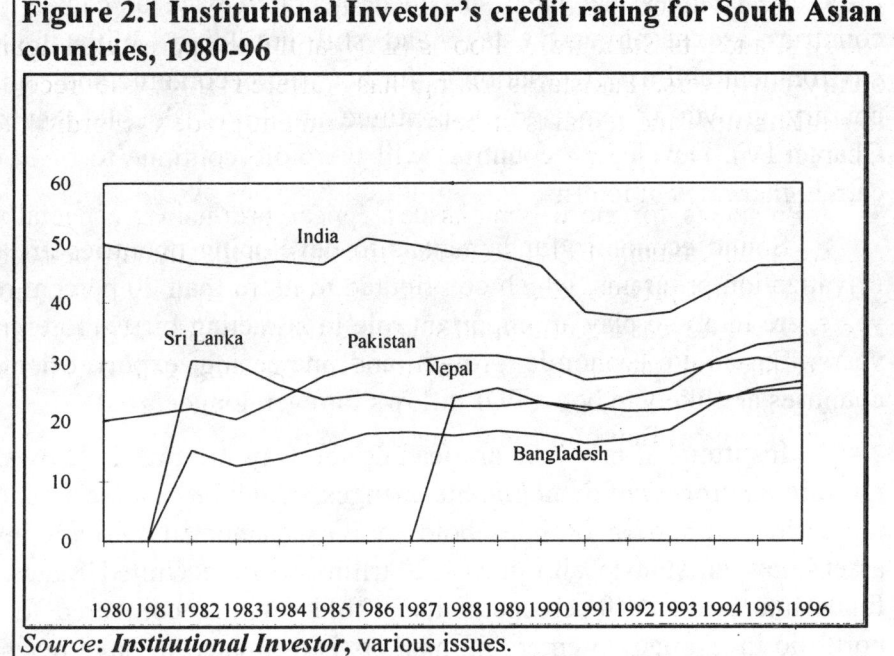

Figure 2.1 Institutional Investor's credit rating for South Asian countries, 1980-96

Source: ***Institutional Investor***, various issues.

As an indicator of financial integration, an Institutional Investor rating below 20 indicates low integration above 50 high integration and, in-between, medium integration (see World Bank 1997).[24] Viewed this way, South Asian countries appear to have improved their degree of financial integration in the 1990s, all reaching the 'medium' level (with India approaching the 'high' category).

Another indication of market credit worthiness is the average spreads on new international bond issues (creditworthiness is associated with an increase in maturity and narrows spreads). In the 1994-96, India launched bond issues on international capital markets at an average spread of 210 basis points and an average maturity of almost 10 years, better than the average terms for developing countries (280 basis points on spreads and eight years maturity). A poor rating for Pakistan resulted in less favorable terms—a spread of 385 basis points with a five year maturity.

---

[24] The same study constructs an index of financial integration, based on the Institutional Investor ratings, the FDI and portfolios ratios to GDP and the level of diversification of a country's financing, based on the composition of private flows. For the period 1992-94, the composite index of financial integration suggests a "high" category for Pakistan; a "medium" for India and Sri Lanka; and a "low" for Bangladesh. If more updated figures covering up to 1996 were used, the index is likely to be changed to: a "high" integration for India and a "medium" for Pakistan.

III. TOWARD SUSTAINED FLOWS AND ENHANCED PRODUCTIVITY

Structural changes that have sustained the rapid pace of capital private flows to developing countries are at an early stage and still unfolding. With the broadly favorable external environment and the expectation of further macroeconomic and regulatory reforms, developing-country growth is expected to continue at almost double that of industrial countries (see Chapter IV). Developing countries will therefore continue to offer investors the opportunity to earn higher rates of return.

Sound economic fundamentals in developing countries are critical to pull investors in. Privatization programs, which contributed to more than 20 percent of entire FDI flows in recent years, are likely to play an important role in attracting bigger foreign investment flows for some years. Sustained economic growth and increasing export orientation in many developing countries are likely to boost FDI inflows for even longer.

Institutional investors are leading the way in portfolio flows. In industrial countries, the reinforcing process of demographic changes, deregulation, and financial innovations results in an increasing proportion of household savings channeled through institutional investors, whose assets now amount to almost US$20 trillion. In the United States, pension funds and mutual funds intermediate 40 percent of household savings, compared to 15 percent in 1975. Global portfolio investment in emerging markets is estimated to have reached US$170 billion in 1995, with the U.S. institutional investors accounting for almost half. The search for higher investment returns and improved portfolio risk management is likely to lead to greater international diversification in emerging markets.

Future prospects for foreign direct and portfolio investment flows to South Asia hinge critically on whether creditworthiness, as well as the business environment can be improved and financial integration increased (see box 2.3).

If South Asian countries sustain and accelerate reforms and increase growth substantially, private capital flows could double or more in the next decade. Cross-country studies indicate that a 1 percentage point increase in the GDP growth rate in the host country could raise FDI inflows by about 10 percent (Jun and Bhasin, 1994).

Besides strengthening macroeconomic fundamentals, South Asian countries need to accelerate trade liberalization, and increase outward orientation of the economy to attract larger capital flows to export sectors. And they could step up the pace of privatization: in 1988-95, the share of South Asia in foreign exchange raised through privatization was less than 2 percent of the total for developing countries, compared with 43 percent in Latin America and 30 percent in Europe and Central Asia. Privatization proceeds could be used to finance critical infrastructure development, and help inject much-needed liquidity to local capital markets. South Asian countries also need to improve institutional and regulatory regimes for FDI, to create an investment environment conducive to more active private-sector (foreign as well as domestic) participation. Despite improvements in recent years in the investment regimes, international investors still find many impediments in the regulatory and business environment (Annex II.III and box 2.3). Finally, financial sector and capital markets reform need to be accelerated to strengthen the capacity of the economy to absorb adverse shocks from volatile portfolio equity flows; improve access to international markets; and strike a better balance between different types of portfolio flows.

Box 2.3 International investors' perceptions of business environment in South Asia

A recent comprehensive survey of leading multinational investors by the European Round Table of Industrialists identifies some remaining impediments.

India. The survey indicated a desire for improved intellectual property rights and less onerous sectoral licensing, as well as further relaxation of ownership restrictions and management control. On general macroeconomic issues, streamlining the tax system and strengthening domestic financial markets were emphasized. Regarding institutional issues, needs for more transparent legal system and greater administrative efficiency were singled out.

Pakistan. Ownership restrictions, performance requirements, and lack of property-right protections led the list of concerns of potential FDI investors. On macro policy issues, protectionism was most frequently cited as a deterrent, followed by a weak tax regime and underdeveloped financial system. Administrative inefficiency was also highlighted as an important issue.

Bangladesh. Investors were mostly concerned about weak macroeconomic conditions and high protectionism. Regarding FDI regimes, intellectual property rights, foreign transaction restrictions, and sectoral licensing were on the high list. As in Pakistan, a weak legal system, administrative inefficiency, and the restricted role of the local private sector drew investor concerns.

Sri Lanka. Most investors considered the country's FDI regime the most liberalized in the region, except for sectoral licensing which still needs to be improved. Concerns were largely on overall macroeconomic environment. As in other countries in the region, multinational enterprises were looking for a more active role of the local private sector.

CHAPTER 3

REGIONAL INTEGRATION

Increased international integration is often accompanied by growing intraregional trade. While intraregional trade in other regions is significant, representing, for example, 40 percent of total trade in East Asia, it accounts for less than 4 percent of the total in South Asia (table 3.1). But official data do not capture the illegal trade between neighbors, which is thought to be substantial. Historically, the modest level of intraregional trade can be explained by protectionist policies and tense political relationships between countries in the region.

Significant progress in liberalizing trade regimes and integrating with the world economy have been made in recent years in all South Asian countries. The region's leaders have intensified regional cooperation in the belief that it will reduce military tensions and stimulate trade and investment. What progress has been made so far in intraregional trade, and what are the potential gains from the establishment of a free trade area?

A conclusion is that such a free trade area would be highly desirable, as long as it is part of a more general strategy of opening up to global competition. Not only the economic gains, as indicated by model simulations, would be significant, particularly for smaller countries. Cooperation and coordinated trade and investment reforms would considerably reduce political and border tensions and make the region a more attractive location for multinational companies and foreign capital. And reduced tensions and settlement of regional disputes could mean big cuts and savings in military spending (which, for example, accounts for 37 percent of public expenditure in Pakistan).

I. INTRAREGIONAL TRADE IN SOUTH ASIA

Intraregional trade: tiny but increasing

Pre-1947, there was substantial trade between what are now India, Pakistan and Bangladesh and Sri Lanka. Some was related to regional differences in resources and climate: Sri Lanka, for example, exported rubber, copra and coconut oil to India, while most jute was farmed in what is now Bangladesh and processed in Bombay. After independence, international trade virtually vanished because of protectionist policies, such as onerous import clearance procedures, high tariffs and import licensing and political factors that made trading relationships difficult.

While a true measurement of intraregional trade is hampered by unreliable data (and unrecorded illegal cross-border trade), the share of official intraregional trade in total trade has been insignificant, at least for the bigger countries. For the region, the share of intraregional trade in total trade has increased modestly from 2.4 percent in 1990 to 3.8 percent in 1996 (table 3.1). India's exports to the rest of South Asia more than trebled in dollar terms between 1990 and 1995—5 percent of total exports. By contrast, India's imports from South Asia grew more slowly and now account for just half a percent of its imports. The growing trade surplus with many of its neighbors is considered an impediment to improving bilateral trade and economic relations.

Table 3.1 Intraregional trade
(in percent)

	Share of intra-regional exports in total exports			Share of intra-regional imports in total imports			Share of intra-regional trade in total trade		
	1990	1995	1996	1990	1995	1996	1990	1995	1996
Bangladesh	3.6	2.7	1.7	6.8	17.6	17.7	5.8	12.8	12.5
India	2.7	5.0	4.8	0.4	0.5	0.4	1.4	2.6	2.4
Nepal	7.2	9.0	11.2	11.7	17.6	21.4	10.2	15.0	18.2
Pakistan	4.0	3.1	2.5	1.6	1.4	2.4	2.6	2.1	2.5
Sri Lanka	3.3	2.4	2.2	6.7	7.8	8.5	5.3	5.8	6.1
South Asia	3.1	4.3	4.0	1.8	3.6	3.6	2.4	3.9	3.8
Sub-Saharan Africa	8.0	11.5	11.3	9.3	11.7	13.0	8.6	11.6	12.2
East Asia and Pcific	33.3	41.6	41.4	32.6	37.9	39.3	32.9	39.7	40.4
NAFTA	41.4	46.2	47.3	33.9	38.4	39.7	37.2	41.9	43.2

Note: For classification of countries within regions, see GEP96.

East Asia also includes Hong Kong, Singapore, and Taiwan.

Source: Direction of Trade Statistics, IMF.

Unofficial trade has flourished

While official trade has been relatively modest, illegal trade has boomed. Hefty profits can be made from contraband trade that circumvents high trade barriers among South Asian countries and complex customs and transit procedures, and exploits different levels of protection vis-à-vis third countries. India has been denying transit facilities to Nepal and Bhutan for exports to Bangladesh, while Bangladesh has denied India transit through its territory to reach India's North-East States. A recent survey of unofficial trade between India and Bangladesh determined that the volume and direction of unrecorded cross-border trade mirrored the pattern of official trade.[25] Illegal imports to Bangladesh (mainly, fruits, vegetables, spices, pharmaceuticals and cattle), was almost equal to the volume of legal imports. Illegal trade undermines the rule of law, leads to losses in tax revenue,[26] and smuggling costs are passed on to consumers. As tariff barriers are steadily reduced and transit rights restored, the incentive for smuggling should diminish. The easing of bilateral border regulations between India, Bangladesh and Nepal would lead not only to an expanded trade and reduced trade imbalances, but also less illegal trade.[27]

Has trade been fostered by regional arrangements?

South Asian Association for Regional Cooperation. An institutional framework for accelerating the process of economic, social and cultural exchanges among South Asian countries was created in 1985, with the South Asian Association for Regional Cooperation (SAARC), followed by the 1993 Preferential Trade Agreement.[28] Initially five areas of cooperation were identified, but

---

[25] See World Bank (1996a).

[26] See World Bank (1995). It estimates Bangladesh's custom revenue loss due to smuggled goods is $94 million, or 3.5 percent of total tax receipts (p 32).

[27] For a discussion of unofficial trade see Raghavan (1995).

[28] For full account of SAARC's objectives see Chapter 2 in Raghavan; SAARC country members are: Bangladesh, Bhutan, India, Maldives, Nepal, Pakistan and Sri Lanka

regional cooperation was confined to areas such as cultural, sports and youth activities. Even now, little has been achieved regarding some core objectives, such as increasing trade and investment and transferring technology, mainly because of still-running political and territorial disputes among members (India and Pakistan, for instance). In response to this slow progress, a deepening of regional economic cooperation was sought as a way to accelerate the pace of integration.

Preferential Trade Agreement. A major initiative promoting greater regional economic cooperation was taken in 1993 with the Preferential Trading Arrangement (SAPTA), which became operational in April 1995 when minor tariff concessions were negotiated. The agreement aims at periodic negotiations for exchange of trade concessions on tariff, para-tariff and nontariff measures. Although it allows for negotiation on a sectoral basis, the approach so far has been to trade concessions on product by product. This is time consuming and ultimately futile as vested interests in member countries exert pressure on government to avoid liberalizing their sector.

Evaluating SAPTA's progress. The first-round exchange of preferences in 1995 were indeed minimal. Concessions resulted in intraregional trade liberalization affecting an estimated 6 percent of traded goods. India's preferential imports under the first round amounted to about US$12 million, more than half of which came from Bangladesh, while India received concessions of roughly $40 million, mainly from Sri Lanka. More significant, the first round did not address non-tariff barriers. The second-round agreement (effective March 1997) concluded seemingly more far-reaching measures with an exchange of preference on around 2000 products.

To evaluate the extent of trade liberalized, Mukherji (1997) compared the concession list against the top fifty products traded among signatories to the agreement 1995-96. (Tables III.4 and III.5 Annex III.I). For example, India offered concessions on 513 items (tariff reductions of 50 percent on 200 items) and agreed to remove quantitative restrictions on 330 items from Bangladesh. In exchange, Bangladesh agreed to a 10 percent reduction on tariffs on 204 items. In the case of India and Bangladesh, however, the bilateral exchange of concessions has been inconsequential as only two low-ranked products among the top fifty traded in Bangladesh were offered concessions. For Pakistan and Sri Lanka, the number of concessions offered was higher, but still limited. On the positive side, the second round of the Preferential Trading Arrangment does at least address some non-tariff measures.

Toward a free trade area?

Regional arrangements are not necessary for economic success or even rapid growth of intra-regional trade. East Asia's phenomenal growth evolved largely independent of special arrangements with industrial countries or with regional integration agreements. Chile and Mauritius are further examples of countries that achieved impressive economic growth based on sound domestic policies and a willingness to exploit opportunities offered by international markets. On the other hand, international experience suggests that preferential trading agreements and regional cooperation can help in so far as they promote greater openness to the world.[29] Even the easing of border restrictions could significantly increase trade. Trade between China and Vietnam, for example, was disrupted by conflict in the late 1970s, but a border trade

---

[29] The literature on regionalism is extensive. See for example R. Lipsey (1957), R. Lawrence (1996), G. Grossman, E. Helpman (1993), J. Frankel (1995), W. Corden (1972), J. Bhagwati (1971), and A.O. Krueger (1995).

protocol renewed in 1988 led to a tenfold increase in trade. Not only did the composition of trade expand beyond the initial limited number of items, but small tariffs have become important sources of revenue for impoverished border areas, and helped to stabilize economic relations between the two countries (Womack, 1994). The flourishing illegal trade among members of the South Asian Association for Regional Cooperation, particularly along the border of Bangladesh and India, is an indication that trade has the potential to increase significantly.

During the 1996 negotiations of the second round commerce ministers expressed a commitment to establish a free trade area no later than 2005. At the ninth summit on regional cooperation held in May 1997, members, recognizing the slow progress in regional integration agreed to advance the deadline for forming a free trade zone to 2000. They also agreed that the next round should provide for deeper tariff concessions and cover products that are actively traded. If carried out, this would represent a vast improvement on the effectiveness of liberalization.

Would the region gain substantially from a free trade area?

Some studies have looked at regional integration in South Asia to determine potential gains. A 1993 World Bank study concluded that, at the time, most of the pre-conditions needed to enhance the probability of a successful free trade Arrangment were not present in South Asia.[30] These are high pre-arrangement tariffs, high level of trade before any arrangement. The existence of complementary rather than competitive trade, and differences in economic structure based on competitiveness. It concluded that South Asia would be better off liberalizing unilaterally and trying to tie up with an established group, such as NAFTA or the European Union.

Levels of trade protection have come down significantly in South Asia since the early 1990s (see Chapter 1). Nominal tariffs, however, are still among the highest of any region, tariff structures are complex and many quantitative restrictions remain. With respect to competitiveness and complementarity, the 1993 World Bank study argued that since South Asian countries are labor abundant with an advantage in labor-intensive manufacturing and export similar goods, they have little incentive to trade. Raghavan (1995) has attempted to evaluate this argument by analyzing South Asia's trade at the 3-digit commodity level (SITCs). He found that less than half of these products were exported by at least two countries; and the number of competing products could be even lower, as the techniques for their identification in the trade statistics do not necessarily capture the quality differences. Moreover, even where there is competition, there are opportunities to convert differences into complementarities by, for example, establishing joint marketing boards for some commodities. In addition to complementarity and levels of protection, trade volumes are another indicator of the potential for a successful arrangement. As already discussed in Chapter 1, they have increased significantly in all South Asian countries in the 1990s.

Empirical research by Srinivasan and Canonero (1993) and Srinivasan (1994) suggested that unilateral trade liberalization, rather than preferential liberalization would yield the greatest trade gain for the region.[31] The small economies of the region, however, would gain more from

---

[30] See J.P. de Melo and D Arvind Rodrik (1993).
[31] See T. N. Srinivasan and G. Canonero (1993) and T.N.Srinivasan (1994).

regional integration than larger economies.[32] They found that potential gains from preferential liberalization, though less than those from unilateral liberalization, are substantial. A simulation using a gravity model shows that the effect of removing all tariffs, combined with the low transport costs, would be to increase total trade between 3 percent of GDP for India to 21 percent for Bangladesh and 59 percent of GDP for Nepal.[33] For a 50 percent tariff reduction, total trade would increase between 0.5 percent of GDP in India and about 9 percent of GDP in Nepal.

II. SIMULATION OF THE BENEFITS FROM PREFERENTIAL LIBERALIZATION

These studies have addressed only the trade impact and not the welfare consequences of preferential and unilateral liberalization. Preferential liberalization may be welfare enhancing even if trade diversion (which occurs as members substitute low cost products from outside with high-cost products from inside the region) is larger than trade creation (as high cost local production is replaced with imports of more efficiently produced goods from the trading partners).[34] Moreover, preferential liberalization may have many noneconomic benefits, particularly social and political, that are difficult to account for in a quantitative way.

To shed some light on these issues, welfare consequences of preferential liberalization can be compared with those of discriminatory liberalization. The analysis was undertaken using the Global Trade Policy Analysis Project (GTAP) model (described in Chapter V.). The model takes into account the production structure of each region of the world, bilateral trade between regions, and major global trade distortions, including tariffs on manufactures, tariff and nontariff barriers on agriculture, and the export quotas imposed under the Multi-fiber Arrangement. The South Asia region is differentiated into India, and the rest of South Asia. Two scenarios are simulated, using tariff levels in the base year, 1992. Under the first, the regional liberalization scenario, all tariffs between these two trading partners are removed while those against the rest of the world remain in place. Under the second, the unilateral liberalization scenario, both India and the rest of South Asia remove all import barriers.

The welfare results imply that regional liberalization generates significant benefits both for India and the rest of South Asia (table 3.2). The welfare gains from regional liberalization are the sum of trade creation benefits (increased trade between countries in

Table 3.2 Welfare consequences of liberalization in South Asia. (in US 1992 dollar)

	India	Rest of South Asia
Regional liberalization	1326	711
(in % of GDP)	(0.5)	(1.0)
Free trade	10943	568
(in % of GDP)	(4.1)	(0.8)

---

[32] Their gains would also be larger than potential gains from liberalizing with other regions, e.g., the European Union For example, if all tariffs were removed with the European Union, total trade would increase by 30.4 percent of GDP in India but only 13.5 percent in Bangladesh and 26 percent in Nepal. For Bangladesh and Nepal these gains are lower than what they could gain by preferential liberalization within the South Asia region.

[33] In this model trade is a function of GDP, GDP per capita, the real exchange rate and the distances of Bombay, Calcutta and Madras from the principal cities of Pakistan, Bangladesh, Sri Lanka and Nepal. The large gains are the result of reduced tariff levels and the very low transport costs in the subcontinent.

[34] Even if trade diversion dominates, internal trade liberalization may induce dynamic effects and economies of scale that result in a higher demand for imports from outside the region. The income effect may outweigh the trade diversion effect, thus increasing global welfare. See J. Bhagwati (1971).

the region) from lower barriers; minus the trade diversion losses caused by replacing non-South Asian imports with now-preferred South Asian goods; plus the terms of trade gains associated with increased access to each other's still-protected markets.

India's gains are much larger in the unilateral liberalization scenario than in the regional scenario. In the latter, trade creation gains are modest because the rest of South Asia is so much smaller, while terms of trade gains are low because protection in the rest of South Asia is also lower than in India. By contrast, the benefits to the rest of South Asia from preferential liberalization are larger than those from unilateral liberalization. This is because the rest of South Asia gains free access to the highly protected Indian market, which results in a significant improvement in terms of trade.[35]

Besides the welfare gains suggested by the simulations, the case for encouraging an intensification of regional cooperation rests on broader considerations. First, it could complement efforts to open up to world competition and make the region a more attractive location for multinational companies and foreign capital. Second, and most important, it is a step towards better political relations—and peace. Additional economic benefits from reduced military spending following settlement of regional disputes could well be substantial.

---

[35] A caveat: the two scenarios were based on the 1992 level of trade protection, which was much higher than now. It is therefore conceivable that the gains from regional liberalization would currently be lower.

CHAPTER 4

THE INTERNATIONAL ECONOMIC ENVIRONMENT

South Asia's rapid export growth in the early 1990s could not have happened without the boom in world trade and reduced protectionism. What kind of external environment will South Asia face in the next ten years? And, will its integration into the world economy and its economic growth accelerate?[36]

The global economic environment in the next decade is expected to be broadly favorable. Industrial country economies are projected to expand steadily, with low inflation but slightly higher real interest rates. Against this background, increasing integration of world production and liberalization of trade regimes will provide the momentum for further expansion in world trade. And the increasing private capital flows to developing countries will reinforce the opportunities for growth.

Such external conditions present exceptional growth opportunities for South Asia. Assuming structural reforms continue South Asian GDP is expected to grow by about 6 percent or so a year, almost one percentage point higher than in the early 1990s. While political instability is a cloud on the horizon, reforms are being pursued (in India and other places) even amid political uncertainty and changes in governments.

South Asia's integration in the global economy, however, is likely to increase its vulnerability to external shocks. Broadly, South Asia's export base is not diversified enough. In some economies, there is heavy concentration in textiles and garments, which is forecast to increase over the coming decade. Export price volatility in agricultural products is decreasing as their share in merchandise trade falls. But South Asia is vulnerable to other commodity price swings—oil prices, for instance, are a particular concern for India and Pakistan.

I. GLOBAL ENVIRONMENT

GDP growth. Developing country GDP is expected to grow at 5.6 percent a year in the next decade, due to the favorable external environment, rapid increases in world trade, low inflation and interest rates, and stepped up reforms. The G-7 countries, the main export markets for developing countries, are projected to grow almost 1 percentage point faster than in the early 1990s—at 2.6 percent a year. Among the major economies, the United States which slipped into shallow recession in 1991, has since registered six years of sustained growth. In the medium term, steady growth of 2.5 percent a year is expected as a result of further fiscal consolidation. After four years of stagnation, the Japanese economy grew by 3.6 percent in 1996, fueled by public—sector spending. Growth may slow in 1997 as fiscal balances are tightened but it is expected to accelerate again after 1998. In Europe, recovery from recession has been delayed because of weak investment demand and shaky confidence. A modest recovery is now underway, however, stimulated by low interest rates and depreciation of the ERM currencies against the dollar.

---

[36] Analysis in this chapter is taken largely from the Global Economic Prospects and the Developing Countries 1997.

Table 4.1. Global Environment
(annual average percentage change)

	1974-80	1981-90	1991-95	1996	1997-06
Real GDP growth					
G-7 countries	2.5	2.9	1.8	2.3	2.6
LMICX[a]	4.6	3.0	4.9	5.4	5.6
Inflation in G-7 Countries[b]	10.1	9.6	2.8	2.1	2.5
Real Export growth					
World	5.0	4.2	6.5	5.5	6.5
LMICX	2.1	2.7	10.0	6.5	7.4
Price indices (US$)					
Export unit value of manufactures (MUV)[c]	11.6	3.3	3.6	-4.2	2.2
Price of petroleum[d]	29.4	-7.7	-8.8	24.1	-3.8
Non-Oil commodity price[d]	-2.2	-5.4	0.5	-1.7	-1.5
Interest rates					
Nominal 6 month US$ LIBOR	9.5	10.0	4.9	5.7	6.2
Real 6 month US$ LIBOR[e]	0.2	5.0	1.7	2.5	3.1

(a) LMICX=Low and middle-income countries excluding Eastern Europe and countries of the former Soviet Union.
(b) Consumer price index in local currency, aggregated using 1988-90 GDP weights.
(c) Data for G-7 countries (Canada, France, Germany, Italy, Japan, the United Kingdom, and the United States) weighted by exports of manufactures to developing countries.
(d) Based on World Bank indices and deflated by export price of manufactures.
(e) Deflated by US CPI.
Source: International Economics Department. Projections are from Global Economic Prospects, May 1997

World trade. Since the mid-1980s, global trade has expanded almost twice as fast as world GDP. Why? Widespread trade liberalization has brought down the median unweighted average tariff (for a sample of 48 developing countries) by 9 percentage points between the mid 1980s and the early 1990s and industrial country tariffs are a third of what they were in the 1960s. Intraregional trade is increasing and communication costs are falling. Private capital flows to developing countries, especially FDI, are booming. Volume growth of world merchandise trade, however, fell in 1996 to 5.5 percent. Several factors were responsible—a fall-off in European import demand; slow growth in import volume in East Asia, where concerns about over-heating in the economy led to monetary tightening in China, Thailand, and Malaysia; and a global downturn in demand for electronics and semiconductors. World trade growth is expected to pick-up again in 1997-98, settling, at 6.4 percent over the next 10 years and, continuing its long-term trend of outstripping output growth.

Prices and interest rates. Price pressures softened in 1996. Inflation is unlikely to pick up in the next few years because of wide output gaps in Japan and many European countries and a firm and coordinated anti-inflation stance by most central banks. Interest rates, however, are likely to increase modestly, as growth revives. Short-term dollar interest rates will average about one percentage point higher than they were in the early 1990s, or roughly 50 basis points above 1996 rates.

The external environment and South Asia

For South Asia, the external environment will likely be positive in 1997-2006. (table 4.2). Trade-weighted growth of merchandise imports of partner countries is estimated at 6 percent a year, higher than in the 1980s and marginally higher than in the early 1990s.[37] Fiscal consolidation and low inflation in industrial countries, as well as improvements in terms of trade will provide a stable environment for accelerating growth in trade and financial integration.

Table 4.2 External environment for South Asia
(annual average percentage change)

	1974-80	1981-90	1991-95	1996	1997-06
Export Market Import gr. a/	5.7	4.8	5.9	5.2	6
Terms of Trade					
LMICs excl. E.Eur & FSU	6.7	-3.2	-2.2	2.1	-0.2
South Asia	-5.6	0.8	1.6	-2.1	0.7
Key Commodity Prices, in real terms					
Rice	-7.6	-7.1	-0.1	10.2	-1.1
Wheat	-7	-5.2	1.8	22.4	-3.8
Tea	-0.3	-4.1	-9	15.5	-0.6
Fertilizers	3.4	-4.8	0.5	7.2	-2.5
Cotton	-5	-4.4	-0.4	-13	-0.9

Source: International Economics Department, February 1997.
Note: Regional projections are taken from GEP97, May 1997.
a/ Import growth of major trading partner weighted by South Asia exports to them.

Better terms of trade. In the next ten years, South Asia can expect a mild improvement in the terms of trade, thanks partly to slower growth of import prices of manufactures. They are projected to increase only modestly—2.3 percent a year (in US$), compared with 3.3 percent in the 1980s. Since almost 80 percent of all imports of South Asia are manufactures, the gain would be substantial. Softer oil prices are also expected to help the terms of trade. The easing of grain prices (wheat 4 percent a year, rice 1.3 percent) should help bring down the cost of food imports for Pakistan and Bangladesh in particular but will also reduce earnings for exporters.

Capital inflows. Prospects for private capital flows are good, if sound macroeconomic environments are maintained and trade and financial sector reforms accelerated. Official development assistance, however, fell from 1.9 percent of South Asia's GDP in 1991 to about 0.7 percent in 1995 as industrial countries tried to reduce fiscal deficits and delayed approving replenishments of the capital of multilateral banks. There is scant hope that they will increase in nominal or real terms in the near future.

II. OUTLOOK FOR SOUTH ASIA

Against the background of a positive external environment, domestic and policy factors will largely determine macroeconomic outcomes in different countries. Projections for South Asia assume continued reforms, justified by recent events that show that the commitment to reforms has grown in all countries, in spite of occasional government changes. In the next decade, South

---

[37] This is slightly less than the growth in world trade because of the growing weight of East Asia in South Asia's exports.

Asia is expected to have higher growth than in the 1980s, the result of a strong supply response of the economy, and increased openness (table 4.3).

Table 4.3 The outlook for South Asia and the developing countries
(annual average percentage change)

Indicator	South Asia				Developing Countries			
	1981-90	1991-95	1996	1997-2006	1981-90	1991-95	1996	1997-2006
Real GDP growth	5.8	4.4	6.5	5.9	2.7	2.3	4.5	5.4
Per capita real GDP growth	3.4	2.5	4.6	4.1	0.7	0.7	2.8	3.8
Real gross domestic investment	6.6	4.9	9.7	9.3	1.2	2.5	6.0	6.7
Export volume (GNFS) growth	5.5	11.4	6.4	10.4	2.2	8.9	5.9	7.2
Deficit as percent of GDP	-8.4	-7.7	-6.8	..	-4.7	-4.4	-2.4	..
Current account deficit as percent of GDP	-3.5	-2.3	-2.5	-2.1	-1.1	-1.7	-1.4	-1.6

Source: IEC, World Bank

GDP growth. For South Asia, GDP growth is projected to accelerate to 5.9 percent in 1997-2006, resulting in a strong increase in real per capita income. After 7 percent GDP growth in 1996 for the third consecutive year, India is likely to outperform other countries in the region, benefiting from a strong supply response of the economy, particularly from private investments. In 1996, Pakistan faced a balance of payments crisis, but the new government elected in early 1997 enjoys strong support and is committed to continued reforms. Bangladesh has been relatively stable since the June 1996 elections but the new government has had limited success in slicing inflation and attracting foreign investors. And it has yet to tackle trickier reforms, such as privatization of loss-making public enterprises.

Export volume growth. South Asia's export growth is likely to remain strong, though less than in the early 1990s. This is because a devaluation of the real exchange rate of the magnitude seen in 1991-93 is unlikely given the adverse effects on inflationary pressures and may even be undesirable with a projected fiscal deficit of roughly 5 percent of GDP. However, export growth will be among the highest in the world, helped by further liberalization of trade regimes and deregulation of domestic markets, expansion of market access for the region's textile and clothing exports (particularly after the MFA is scrapped), and a slowdown of exports and GDP growth in China and East Asia. Increased intraregional trade may also play a part if the South Asia Preferential Trade Agreement is implemented.

While prospects for South Asia are favorable, there are many major challenges, particularly the reduction in the fiscal deficit. This task is complicated by minimum revenue collections, widespread tax evasion and high spending on defense. Fiscal imbalances will continue to run in tandem with large current account deficits, increasing South Asia's vulnerability to external shocks. Current account deficits are (and are expected to remain) large particularly in Nepal, Pakistan and Bangladesh, while in India, they are projected to remain below 2 percent.

III. CURRENT ACCOUNT VULNERABILITIES

Despite the positive external outlook, increased integration of South Asia in the world economy may increase exposure to shocks. These are underscored by the massive concentration of merchandise exports in textiles and garments in most countries (less so in India), high reliance on imported energy (for India and Pakistan) and susceptibility to changes in international interest rates and exchange rates and volatility in private capital flows.

Supply shocks: agriculture

In agriculture, the region is exposed to commodity price swings. Table 4.4 shows that in the past export price volatility has been significantly greater in Sri Lanka and Pakistan than the average for all developing countries in the Asia-Pacific region. Vulnerability to changes in prices of food imports is also a problem particularly for Bangladesh, Sri Lanka, and Nepal, which are net food importers. Projected trend decline in cereal prices may decrease vulnerability.

Table 4.4 Export price volatility, 1948-1991

Region Country	Percent of World
India	296
Pakistan	680
Sri Lanka	504
Philippines	797
Thailand	572
Indonesia	414
LMICx (Asia-Pac)	145
World	100

Note: Volatility is measured as the export-weighted sum of commodity price variances.
Source: International Economic Dept. 1994

Merchandise exports. A poorly diversified export base (in products or markets) leaves a country vulnerable to cyclical downturns. The region is highly (even overly) dependent on textiles and garments which in some countries account for more up to 75 percent of export revenue. In Pakistan the concentration on exports of cotton fiber, fabric and garments exports leaves the sector not only vulnerable to swings in cotton prices but to production failures from, for instance, drought, disease and pests. In Nepal, the situation is even more precarious with just one product, carpets, accounting for half of all merchandise earnings.

Oil imports. Vulnerability to oil price and supply shocks is of particular concern to India and Pakistan, having prompted all of India's last three balance-of-payments crises. Higher international crude prices in 1996 quickly racked up the import bill for petroleum and petroleum products in India and Pakistan. The future looks a little different, however. Current baseline projection are for declining long-run world oil prices [by around 3.8% a year] in real terms during the next decade, a result of increased efficiency in both production and consumption and increased supply from non-OPEC producers.

South Asian oil imports in 1996 represented a quarter of merchandise export earnings. The projected fall in oil prices from 1996 levels would save about $1.4 billion a year in current dollars. Trends for India's oil import demand, however, suggest that it will grow substantially in the coming decade, so that India's vulnerability to unexpected rises in oil prices is likely to increase.[38] On the other hand, weak real oil prices mean that prospects for workers remittances are poor as many South Asian emigrants are working in oil exporting countries.

Interest rates. A rise in foreign interest rates can affect the balance of payments directly by raising interest payments, and potentially can affect creditworthiness or can prompt capital outflows. Although the interest rate outlook for South Asia is favorable, with an expected average real interest rate of 3.1 percent in the forecast period, this does not preclude cyclical or

---

[38] See *India in the Global Economy*, Policy Research Working Paper No 1681, World Bank, 1996.

other interest rate movements of the kind that contributed to precipitating the Mexican crisis in 1994. Of the region's US$161 billion in external debt (at the end of 1996) less than 20 percent is variable rate and sensitive to movements in international trade (compared with 52 percent for the LAC region, for example). However, this share has been rising from a low of 3 percent in 1980, and the trend is expected to continue. So far, all countries in the region have managed to avoid debt restructuring. Debt indicators are relatively high but improving: the debt to export ratio has fallen to 209 percent in 1996 (from about 219 percent in 1995); the ratio of debt to GNP fell to about 28 percent and the ratio of debt service to exports to 23 percent in 1996, down from 31 percent and 25 percent in 1995 respectively.[39]

The decline in concessional lending and the rise in variable rate long-term debt has affected mainly India and Pakistan. For these countries, declines in shares of bilateral grants and concessional lending have been offset by an increase in official non-concessional lending and private flows. Estimates suggest that, within five years, net flows from official sources may be negligible as grants stagnate or decline and funding from multilateral organizations decreases, a trend that reflects fiscal tightening in donor countries. The expected greater variability of debt servicing costs will raise the premium on improving debt servicing capacity, particularly on achieving a large and fast growing export base.

---

[39] In Pakistan, however, in 1996 the debt to export ratio rose to 270 percent from 258 percent in 1995 and the debt service ratio rose to 29 percent, the highest in the region. The highest debt to export ratio is in Bangladesh (292 percent) while debt to GNP ratios range from 26 percent in India to 62 percent in Sri Lanka.

CHAPTER 5

PROSPECTS FOR SOUTH ASIAN EXPORTS
EMPHASIZING TEXTILES AND CLOTHING

While the external environment for developing countries in the medium term is expected to remain favorable, the performance of each country will depend on the interaction of various forces, including population growth, capital and skills, market opportunities created by expanding world trade and falling transport and communications costs, as well as the pace of trade liberalization and reforms to increase competitiveness.

Using an integrated general equilibrium model of the world economy (the Global Trade Policy Analysis Project or GTAP), it is possible to assess how these forces will affect South Asian exports in the next quarter century. The assumptions of the model are consistent with those adopted in *Global Economic Prospects 1997*, and include the full implementation of the Uruguay Round, inclusion of China in the World Trade Organization and the abolition of the Multi-Fibre Arrangement (MFA) in 2005. Particularly, the focus is on the trade and welfare impact of two important policy changes—the phasing out of export quotas on textiles and clothing imposed under the MFA and reduction in trade protection in South Asian countries in the 1990s.

The simulation results are illustrative rather than projections. So, what do they show?

- South Asia emerges as a major force in world trade in the next 25 years. Annual growth of exports in 1992-2020 will outpace that of output in both India and the rest of South Asia. With almost 12 percent a year, India will experience the highest export growth in the world (though its share in world exports will only reach 4 percent in 2020, up from less than 1 percent in 1992). In less efficient countries of South Asia, exports will grow more slowly (7.5 percent a year) about the same as other developing countries. Underlying this performance are two major policy changes— the dramatic reductions in trade protection in South Asia and the abolition of the Multi-Fiber Arrangement (MFA). Both have contributed to increasing economic efficiency and integration with the global economy. Abolition of the MFA alone means significant growth in exports of textiles and clothing but the gains are even higher if a package of reforms to raise productivity in the clothing sector is implemented. South Asia's trade liberalization also increases exports of other manufactures, contributing to diversification of the region's export base. Both reforms generate substantial increases in real income.

- Specialization in India is different to the rest of South Asia. The next 25 years will bring about not only a significant improvement in exports and output of South Asia but a marked change in specialization in India. India's comparative advantages will shift from labor-intensive to more capital-and-skills intensive sectors, such as light and heavy manufactures and machinery and equipment. By 2020, these three sectors will account for 64 percent of exports, compared with 28 percent in 1992, while apparel and textile exports will be less than 13 percent of exports, half of the level in 1992. The comparative advantages of the rest of South Asia will remain in labor-intensive products and textile and apparel will continue to account for about half of the region's exports. But even these countries will have a more diversified export structure, with an increasing share of light manufactures and primary agriculture products.

The plan of the chapter is as follows. Given the importance of textile and apparel in South Asian exports, section I describes the nature of the MFA regulations, its current impact on South Asia's exports, and the expected benefits from its phasing out. Section II reports the simulations of export growth and export structure, which cover the period from the benchmark year (1992) to 2020. Section III illustrates the welfare gains of removing the MFA. The impacts on output and exports of two policy reforms are then simulated: *first*, the introduction of a package of reforms that raises labor productivity in South Asia to the current level of productivity in China (section IV); *second*, the trade liberalization occurring in India during 1991-98, since India is the only country for which detailed information is available on protection, at the sector level (section V).

I. MULTI-FIBRE ARRANGEMENT: BENEFITS FROM ABOLITION

The Multi-Fibre Arrangement (MFA), introduced in the early 1970s, is essentially an "arrangement" by which industrial countries imposed import quotas on exports of textiles and clothing of developing countries. The Agreement on Textiles and Clothing of 1994 provides for a ten-year phasing out of all MFA quotas by the year 2005 (Box 5.1).

As with any trade restraint, MFA quotas create costs for both exporters and importers. They are usually negotiated bilaterally and governments of exporting countries can (and occasionally do) sell the quotas through auction or allocate them according to pre-set rules. In South Asia, quotas are according to past export performance, thus creating incentives for inefficient export levels that are likely to lead to substantial economic costs (Trela and Whalley 1995). Quotas also lead to lower prices in unrestricted markets because of excess supply. And as quotas divert output from low to high-cost producers, they tend to increase the average cost of world textiles.

Box 5.1 The MFA and the Agreement on Textiles and Clothing

The 1994 Uruguay Round Agreement on Textiles and Clothing provided for the phase-out of non-tariff restrictions under the Multi Fiber Agreement over 10 years in four stages—on January 1995, 1998, 2002 and 2005. Products accounting for 16 percent of 1990 imports were integrated under GATT rules in 1995, 17 percent will be integrated in 1998 and 18 percent in 2002. The program has been implemented in a way that leaves most adjustments until the end of the 10 years (49 percent of textile and clothing products, including the most seriously restricted products, will not be fully integrated into the GATT until 2005). The acceleration in the growth of export quotas represents a significant expansion in market access opportunities for developing countries. Moreover, for products under bilateral restraint, the agreement provides for progressively increasing existing growth rates. Quota growth for many of the products exported by South Asian countries are expected to increase to more than 11 percent a year by the end of the implementation period.

The expected gains from the elimination of quotas (price increases in unrestricted markets and greater efficiency in production) depend on a number of factors. These include the share of exports to quota and non-quota markets, quota rents enjoyed in restricted markets, and restrictiveness of quotas, as measured by export-tax equivalents.[40] Efficiency of South Asian countries relative to competitors and their ability to expand production and exports must also be taken into account.

Share of exports to quota and non-quota markets.[41] Quota abolition lowers prices in the previously protected markets, and raises prices in once unprotected markets. In general, countries with exports directed mainly to protected markets tend to enjoy high quota rents, which will be lost when the MFA is scrapped and prices fall, while countries with large shares directed to unrestricted markets are likely to as prices rise. In South Asia, between 30 percent and 50 percent of textile exports go to quota markets, as do 75 percent of apparel exports (Annex IV.I).

Export tax equivalents. To export, a firm needs to obtain quotas by administrative decision, by purchase (if the quota rights are tradable), barter, or it has to accept a lower price as a sub-contractor to a quota holder. Whatever the approach used the MFA quota system introduces a cost analogous to a tax on exports to restricted markets. The higher the export tax equivalent applying to a country, the greater the disincentive created for exports to the restricted market, and the greater the efficiency costs resulting from diversion of productive resources out of their most efficient use, and from distortions of consumer choices.

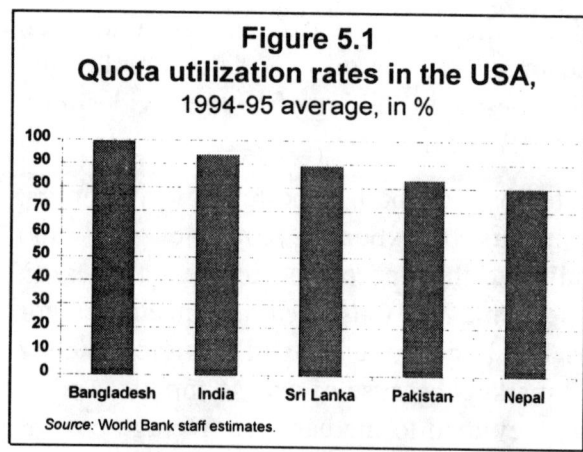

Figure 5.1
Quota utilization rates in the USA,
1994-95 average, in %

Source: World Bank staff estimates.

Where export tax equivalents are not available, as for all South Asian countries other than India,[42] the quota utilization rate provides a useful indicator of the extent to which exports are restricted. In theory, quotas would be filled whenever there are any exports directed to non-quota markets. In practice, this is not necessarily so, since quotas are broken up into relatively finely specified categories. Some quotas may be unfilled while others are tightly restricted. Generally, however, the more restrictive the quotas the higher their utilization is likely to be. Overall, available evidence on the tightness of quota restrictions suggests that Bangladesh and India are the most tightly restricted of South Asian countries (figure 5.1).

---

[40] See Elbeheri, Hertel and Martin (1997).

[41] Export tax equivalents are defined as the percentage increase in the price that the importer is willing to pay over and above the price that would have prevailed without quotas. They have been calculated as follows: ETE = QP/(UV-QP), where QP is the price of the export quota, and UV is the (quota-premium inclusive) export price of the good. The ETE indicates the quota premium as a percentage of the premium less unit value of exports.

[42] Detailed estimates of the export tax equivalents of the textile and clothing quotas for India have been prepared using extensive field interviews for a study undertaken by Kathuria and Bharwaj (1997), and were used as the basis for the analysis. In the absence of comparable high-quality data, the export tax equivalents for the rest of South Asia had to be inferred from information such as quota utilization rates and the coverage of quotas. Because some important markets for other South Asian suppliers are not subject to restrictions (e.g., exports from Bangladesh to the EU), and because of the generally lower level of quota utilization in other South Asian suppliers, the export tax equivalents of the quotas were set around 20 percent below the corresponding rates for India.

II. SIMULATIONS OF EXPORT GROWTH AND CHANGES IN EXPORT STRUCTURE

Export growth simulations were prepared using a multi-country general equilibrium model of the world economy (the Global Trade Policy Analysis Project-the GTAP model, see Annex IV.II). The model includes the World Bank's latest macroeconomic projections. The model also takes into account worldwide policy changes, such as of the Uruguay Round, phasing out the MFA, liberalization of the Chinese economy, and developments in South Asia, such as trade liberalization implemented up to 1997, and the Indo-US and Indo-EU 1996 agreements.[43] The simulations are consistent with the experiments carried out in *Global Economic Prospects 1997*, aimed at evaluating the impact on the world economy of the increased integration of Big 5—China, India, Brazil, Indonesia and Russia.

The results suggest a high growth in export volumes between 1992 and 2005—more than 14 percent a year for India, and 8 percent for the rest of South Asia. This growth is driven by two factors—the relatively high projected economic growth (5.4 percent a year in India and 4.7 percent in the rest of South Asia) and, most important, dramatic improvements in efficiency from trade and price liberalization. Quotas remain a serious obstacle to expansion of the textile and clothing exports, despite increases in quotas provided under the Uruguay Round.[44] This is relatively more important for India, where growth for these goods fall substantially below overall growth rates.

Table 5.1 Annual Percentage Changes in Export Volumes
(percent)

Sector	1992-2005(pre-MFA abolition)		1992-2020	
	India	Rest of South Asia	India	Rest of South Asia
Primary agriculture	6.6	8.3	9.4	8.9
Processed food	15.9	6.1	11	6.3
Oil and gas	12.3	12.7	19.7	27.3
Other energy	15.9	12.2	14.1	9.7
Other natural resources	8.8	11	7.7	5.7
Textiles	7.3	7.7	7.2	6.8
Apparel	9.6	8.3	10.5	7.4
Light manufactures	18.3	11.1	13.5	8.5
Heavy Manufactures	18.4	10	13.2	9.6
Machinery & Equipment	26.9	14.3	18.8	10.5
Utilities, Housing, Construction	12.5	6.8	6.3	4.2
Other Services	9.6	7.4	4.5	3.1
TOTAL	14.3	8.3	11.7	7.5

Source: World Bank staff estimates.

---

[43] In these agreements the US and the EU committed to early abolition of selected MFA quotas while India committed to a phased removal of quantitative restrictions on imports of fibers, yarn, fabric and apparel as well as lowering import tariffs on textile and clothing.

[44] The administration of the quotas has become more restrictive in recent years and it is assumed that exports from South Asia are constrained by quota growth rates.

For the rest of South Asia, exports of these products are less constrained because quotas are generally less constraining and underlying growth in their exports lower. Generally, exports of light manufactures, machinery and equipment, and heavy manufactures all expand relatively rapidly in all countries in the region. These are relatively capital-intensive goods, and benefit from increases in physical and human capital per worker. Import-intensive manufactures for export production benefit substantially from the rapid trade liberalization.

The elimination of the MFA quotas leads to a marked one-off increase in exports of textiles and clothing from India and the rest of South Asia, (Table 5.2.).[45] This surge compensates substantially for slower growth in the preceding years. As long as the commitment to abolish MFA remains credible, some investments needed to take advantage of a quota-free environment will have been undertaken ahead of abolition, and expansion of exports is likely to occur rapidly.

Table 5.2. Impact of MFA abolition on export volume, %.

	India	Rest of South Asia
Textiles	67	13
Clothing	232	122

Up to 2020, export growth declines slightly. This reflects an inevitable slowdown in trade liberalization; reductions in import costs at the rate achieved in the 1990s simply cannot be maintained. In the rest of South Asia, export growth remains close to that of all developing countries (8.1 percent), though outpacing output growth (5.2 percent). In India, export growth, at 12 percent, is higher than China (10 percent) or in any other region of the world and much higher than output growth (5.8 percent). There are larger increases in export volumes of goods such as machinery and equipment that benefit from the accumulation of physical and human capital (and increases in capital and skills per worker) and from continuing trade liberalization and declining transport costs.

Changes in export structure

The composition and structure of exports also change (Table 5.3). While the simulation captures broad trends—for example the shift in comparative advantages out of textiles and apparel for India and improved export diversification for the rest of South Asia—some qualitative trends of some subsectors (fish and seafood, gems and jewelry, machinery and equipment, software and so on) are emerging (Box 5.2).

---

[45] Notice that the effect of the MFA removal is the result of a comparative static experiment in which the model is given a "shock", by eliminating all quotas, and then a new equilibrium solution is computed. The time horizon has to be considered long enough for all the dynamic adjustments to occur.

Table 5.3 Commodity shares in South Asia exports
(percent)

Sector	India				Rest of South Asia			
	1992	2005 Pre-MFA Abolition	2005 Post-MFA Abolition	2020	1992	2005 Pre-MFA Abolition	2005 Post-MFA Abolition	2020
Primary agriculture	5.9	2.6	2.1	3.2	9.8	10.5	8.4	13.2
Processed food	9.6	11.2	9.6	8.2	6.1	4.7	3.4	5.5
Oil and gas	0.2	0.2	0.2	2.2	0.2	0.5	0.3	1.5
Other energy	1.9	2.4	2.2	1.6	0.3	0.5	0.4	0.3
Other natural resources	16.5	9.6	8.6	5.5	1.7	2.5	1.8	1
Textiles	12	5.3	7.8	3.8	24.5	22.2	21.6	22.6
Apparel	11.7	6.7	18.5	8.8	22.5	22.3	37.7	25.3
Light manufactures	11	15.8	13.1	16.8	7.8	10.6	7.5	12.5
Heavy manufactures	10	14.2	12.3	12.6	1.3	1.6	1.2	2.6
Machinery and equipment	6.6	23.1	18.3	34.4	1.7	3.4	2.3	4.5
Utilities and construction	0	0	0	0	0.1	0.1	0	0
Other services	14.4	8.9	7.4	2.9	23.8	21.1	15.3	11
Total	100	100	100	100	100	100	100	100

Source: World Bank staff estimates.

In India, exports in 1992 were widely diversified; in the rest of South Asia, they were heavily concentrated in textiles, clothing and services. The abolition of quotas in 2005 results in a dramatic expansion of apparel exports in all countries of the region, as they take advantage of their strong comparative advantage. The share of apparel in exports of South Asia reach their peak following the abolition of quotas. Over the period 2005 to 2020, however, the importance of textiles and clothing in India's exports declines sharply as its comparative advantage shifts into light manufactures, and particularly transport machinery and equipment. In the rest of South Asia, there is a hefty decline in the importance of apparel, while more capital-intensive textiles sector continues to increase export share. The importance of primary agriculture and of light manufactures increases, helping to diversify their export bases.

Box 5.2 Prospects for some export subsectors—a qualitative assessment

Fish and seafood. A growing and promising export for some South Asian countries is fish and seafood (currently accounting for about 3 percent of merchandise export earnings in India and 8 percent in Bangladesh). Indian seafood exports, of which roughly half are harvested shrimp, have grown rapidly since the late 1980s and have become the largest agricultural export. India has started to produce cultivated shrimp (20-30 percent of exports) and has diversified into finfish and more recently, freshwater fish such as carp. In Bangladesh, shrimp for export are almost exclusively farmed and have increased significantly in the 1980s and 1990s. Demand for frozen and fresh seafood products in the US, EU and East Asian markets has been rising steadily and is expected to grow fast. Environmental concerns over the inadvertent capture of turtles in shrimp nets, however, could adversely affect India's exports to the US. Opportunities for exports to the EU will continue to grow as new policy measures further reduce the EU's allowable domestic catch. Shrimp consumption in the past five years has expanded beyond traditional markets in North America, the EU and Japan to new markets in Asia, due in part to increasing disposable incomes and abolition of import restrictions by some countries, particularly Taiwan and Korea. Bangladesh and India are well placed to benefit from expansion in demand as their labor costs are much lower than major competitors, such as Thailand. There are, however, potential problems, particularly environmental concerns. A recent cost-benefit analysis commissioned by the Indian Supreme Court, for example, concluded that shrimp farms in two states caused more economic harm than good because of social and environmental costs. And in Bangladesh, where high population densities put pressure on land use, shrimp ponds have displaced rice cultivation in some areas.

Gems and Jewelry Gems and jewelry (which in Tables 5.1 and 5.3 are included in the "natural resources" sector) represent one of the most dynamic exports for India (about 10 percent of merchandise exports) growing at double digit rates since the 1980s. Despite a cyclical downturn in 1996, demand is expected to remain buoyant and the sector competitive. Currently 86 percent of industry exports are low-quality small diamonds (.2 carats and smaller), where India has established itself as a dominant producer and the world's largest 'sight holder' with 40 of the 160 companies that ensure a steady supply of roughs at cheaper prices. Market entry in this end of the industry where capital to labor ratios are low however, is relatively easy and India will be faced with more competition, particularly from Thailand, Malaysia, Indonesia, and China. India is diversifying into higher value-added sectors, such as the design and manufacture of gem studded jewelry where it has just 1.5 percent of the market, but its exports have been growing at 20-30 percent a year over the past decade. Diversification into larger gemstones with more carats would also help India increase its share of the world market. But cutting these larger stones requires modern, automated machinery which is found in only 10 percent of firms. India will have to increase investment in new plant and equipment significantly to compete with the traditional cutting and polishing centers in Tel Aviv, Antwerp and New York where salaries and productivity are higher.

Machinery and equipment While this is not currently one of the top export sectors, it is expected to gain most in the next 20 years as it makes intensive use of the physical and human capital that are projected to grow relatively fast. (*Road vehicles* and *auto parts* are among the most dynamic components). In the past three years especially, growth has been rapid, a trend expected to continue especially in the automotive components sub-sector. This is based on: the globalization and the growing presence of firms such as Toyota, Nissan, Mitsubishi, General Motors and many other multinationals in India; and quality improvements in many Indian firms which have received ISO 9000 certifications. Exports have been boosted by the increasing number of alliances and technical collaboration agreements and many parts producers have entered into joint ventures to secure capital for modernization and expansion. Nonetheless, the industry has a long way to go. It continues to be dominated by thousands of smaller suppliers with dated technology and low inefficient output

Software Within the service sector, one of the most dynamic components in India is software. India's exports of software have grown from $25 million in 1985 to about $600 million by 1996 (though still only 1.3 percent of current-account revenues in 1996). India's particular advantages are its large pool of English-speaking labor, and low labor costs, though they are offset by poor infrastructure and low availability of the latest hardware. India's software exports are still largely concentrated in on-site programming (contract work at clients' premises), a segment with low-value added and low entry barriers in terms of capital and marketing skills. Hence, the rate of assimilation and diffusion of information technology throughout India has been slow. Contract work will decline as data communication links improve and as more off-shore clients feel comfortable outsourcing complete custom-made software projects to firms in India. Value addition and profitability are higher in the custom-made sector as are the benefits from skills transfer, particularly from project management. Shifting to custom-made software for off-shore clients and the development of packaged software will help India to sustain a competitive advantage in the future.

III. WELFARE GAINS FROM MFA ABOLITION

Gains to South Asian countries from phasing out the MFA are expected to be great, because they are severely constrained by the quotas and they are among the lowest cost producers.[46] In fact,

---

[46] See, for example, Kathuria and Bhardwaj (1997) and Kurt Salmon Associates (1995).

many major exporting regions will benefit, and others lose.[47] Gains to India are substantial, particularly in the most constrained apparel sector. This is because its exports are restricted in both the US and the EU markets, and its quota coverage and quota utilization rates are high. India's recent trade liberalization also has a dramatic effect on competitiveness (the average import weighted tariff rate fell from 87 percent percent in 1990-91 to 20.3 percent in 1997-98) as well as deregulation of the man-made fibers sector. For example, the average consumer price of synthetic fibers fell from 740 percent above world prices in 1985 to only 30 percent above in 1995, while producer prices fell from 290 percent above to 30 percent. While protection for these fibers remains high by world standards, it is well below that of a decade ago. Reforms have already resulted in a sixfold increase in output of man-made fibers, and can be expected to contribute to development of broader-based textiles and clothing. High growth in income and investment is projected during the MFA phase out and India's textile and apparel exports are likely to grow rapidly. While its quotas will grow by 115 percent a year to the United States and 91 percent to the EU over 1994 and 2004 because of the Agreement on Textiles and Clothing, even this is not expected to be fast enough to keep up with output growth. As a result, the quotas are likely to become more restrictive.

Other South Asian countries also benefit from abolition of quotas, but less so, as they are typically less-restricted suppliers. While export increases are smaller than in India, output changes needed to achieve these increases are similar. This is because the textile and clothing industries in these countries are more strongly oriented to the export market, and therefore a larger percentage change in output is required to accommodate any given percentage change in exports.

China and the ASEAN countries are also substantial gainers, while the newly industrialized economies lose from MFA abolition. The other gainers are, like India, low cost and tightly restricted suppliers. The newly industrialized countries are, by 2005, relatively high cost producers, whose historically large quotas provide quota rents that slow down restructuring of these sunset industries.

The broad pattern of results in Table 5.4 is consistent with those obtained in earlier studies that analyzed the consequences of abolishing the MFA (see Yang, Martin and Yanagishima 1996; Harrison, Rutherford and Tarr 1996; Hertel, Martin, Yanagishima and Dimaranan 1996), although these studies were conducted without the benefit of the comprehensive and up-to-date estimates of the export tax equivalents used in this report.

---

[47] For importers, there is no such uncertainty. These countries, which curiously imposed these measures, tend to benefit substantially from abolition (see Martin and Winters 1996 for a number of studies that confirm this result).

Table 5.4 Impact of MFA abolition in 2005
(% change over 1992)

	India	Rest of South Asia	NIEs	ASEAN	China
Output (% change)					
Textiles	15.1	12.5	10.1	39.9	17.2
Apparel	114.1	94.7	-22.9	93.4	54.2
Exports (% change)					
Textiles	66.8	13	16.3	19.3	26
Apparel	231.7	121.6	-30.8	152.9	74.3
Real income	1741.2	117.1	-1603.4	1669.3	6440.1
$ US Mill. % of 2005 GDP	0.37	0.9	-0.14	0.24	0.72

Source: World Bank staff estimates.

Why does the rest of South Asia gain less than India? Because, on average, it is less tightly restricted (lower export tax equivalents), and because exports from South Asia are more heavily oriented to the MFA-restricted import markets.

Bangladesh is expected to gain substantially in the US market before 2005, a result of higher growth in quota rates, but will probably lose in the European market because of competition from countries whose quotas grow faster. Moreover, Bangladesh may be hurt by prospective changes in rules of origin.[48] Despite having the strongest revealed comparative advantage in ready-made garments of any South Asian country, Bangladesh has a relatively inward-looking textile sector (see Annex V.I).[49] Textile production is more capital-intensive than clothing and it may be some time before Bangladesh can develop a modern textile sector. Thus, while ensuring a good enabling environment for a competitive textile sector, Bangladesh should allow the apparel industry to source its inputs efficiently cheaper fabrics from India and China, and high-quality fabrics from Japan, Germany and the USA.[50]

Sri Lanka's industry is focused on low-and medium-priced garments. It is competitive because of its low-priced labor, its ability to source inputs at lowest cost world-wide (90 percent of fabric imports are from Asia) and its modern factory-based structure (see Selegama (1996)).

---

[48] Rules of origin requirements were developed to deal with the incentives for transhipment and fraud created by MFA restrictions. In particular, they apply within the GSP (Generalized System of Preferences), a system that allows duty-free entry of many products from least-developed countries into the European Union. In the current scheme (January 1995-January 1998), the criterion for determining origin is the change of heading, e.g. that the good be processed sufficiently for the tariff heading of the output to be different from that of the input. Recent proposals for stricter rules of origin would require that goods be produced using either fabric produced in the exporting country, or in the EU. This would represent a major problem for least-developed countries like Bangladesh that do not appear to have a comparative advantage in the more capital-intensive textile sector. And even if Bangladesh greatly strengthened its textile sector, this requirement would restrict its clothing exports to a relatively narrow range of products that could be fabricated from local cloth, rather than from the best cloth available worldwide. Requiring Bangladesh to use EU cloth would similarly narrow the range of products that it could export successfully.

[49] See UNIDO (1993).

[50] See Selegama (1995).

While quota utilization rates are high, however, it is almost completely focused on MFA quota markets. The increase in growth rates under the Agreement on Textiles and Clothing (by 152 percent in Europe and 121 percent in the USA in 1994-2004) will increase market access. But Sri Lanka may lose income from the abolition of the MFA. It will certainly lose quota rents on its exports and may not be able to benefit sufficiently from higher prices in other markets and from increased efficiency at home to make up the difference.

Pakistan The strong dependence of Pakistan exports of textiles and clothing on its cotton resource base is a strength—and a weakness. The spinning and weaving industries appear to be efficient but they rely heavily on the artificially low producer prices for cotton, about two-thirds of the world price.[51] Pakistan's quota utilization rate, however, was significantly below that in India and Bangladesh in 1994-95, the result of a steep decline in cotton production. While the underlying comparative advantage of Pakistan in cotton, textiles and clothing is strong, future gains will depend on its cotton policies (liberalization of producer prices, tariff reductions and export quotas and soon), as much as abolition of the MFA.

IV. PRODUCTIVITY IMPROVEMENTS IN THE APPAREL SECTOR

Textile and apparel in South Asia have enormous potential given the large pool of low-cost labor. Despite recent reforms, development of these industries is hampered by some policy constraints. In India, these include the reserving of important sub-sectors for small-scale household handloom production, protection and taxation of man-made fibers, obligations to produce particular products (such as hank yarn), and administrative and compliance costs in export credit and duty drawback schemes (see Box 5.3, taken from Kathuria 1997). Some of the same restrictive production policies are reported in Pakistan, while the more export-oriented sectors of Sri Lanka and Bangladesh appear to face fewer constraints.

Box 5.3 India—Policy restrictions on the textile and garment industry

Policy bias towards cotton and against synthetic fibers. Export controls keep prices of raw cotton below the international prices and import duties on synthetic yarn and intermediates are still high. (Customs duties on the most important synthetic fibers, however, now average 20-45 percent, down from 60-200 percent in 1987.) Excise duties on cotton are low.

Policy bias to promote the handloom sector. Promotion of the handloom sector has been a central feature of textile policy in India (it provides employment for about three million weaver households). This has been achieved by restrictions on foreign investments in the clothing sector, the reserving of 22 textile articles exclusively for handloom production and the yank yarn obligation, according to which spinning mills must supply not less than 50 percent of their yarn in the form of hanks for use in the handloom sector (hank yarn is also exempted from excise and sales tax). The combination of these and other restrictions, including labor legislation and lack of an effective exit policy, appear to have seriously held back development of a modern, factory-based system and have caused India to rely heavily upon subcontracting.[52] While this has had some advantages—flexibility of production, cheap labor in the subcontract firms—that have guaranteed the success of garment exports, this decentralized system is a constraint to investment and increased productivity and growth in the future.

Trade policies and procedures. With the easing of trade restrictions and the bilateral treaties with the US and EU signed in 1993, imports of raw cotton, yarn, and selected fabric have been freed. Tariffs have come down and are

---

[51] See Ingco and Winters (1996).
[52] See Kathuria (1997).

slated to fall further. But there are still long-winded administrative procedures for importing and exporting. Nair and Kaul (1996) point out that it takes a staggering nine months for a law-abiding firm to grind through procedures associated with the Advance License—ironically, a system introduced to reduce constraints on exporters. In today's business environment of just-in-time delivery, such procedures are deadly for firms' ability to compete in the world market. The urgency of reform will be greater in the more competitive post-reform environment and benefits correspondingly greater.

Improving competitiveness of the textile and garment sectors. With the MFA to be phased out in 2005, India must prepare for a more competitive environment, both in domestic and foreign markets. The domination by India of market niches, which is based on cheap and flexible labor and raw cotton, is unlikely to last forever. Much of the industry is aware that more factory investment is needed, but has been unwilling to make it, mainly because of the policy constraints. To help, the government can take several steps. First, abolish the laws and regulations that favor small-scale industry in the garment sector, as recommended by the recent Abid Husain Committee. Second, introduce a policy whereby labor can be retrenched if necessary, with appropriate safeguards. Third, include the garment industry on the list of industries for automatic approval for foreign direct investment (up to 51 percent foreign equity.) Fourth, make imported fabrics available for export production, reducing delays in shipments, clearance and so on. Fifth, remove the policy bias (in the form of high taxation) against synthetic fibers.

Table 5.5 illustrates the expected impact of reforms to raise the productivity of labor in the apparel sector[53] from India's level in the early 1990s to the level achieved by China during the same period (Elbeheri, Hertel and Martin 1996)—a shock that involves a 67 percent increase in labor productivity. A similar shock is applied to the rest of South Asia.

Table 5.5 Impact of prospective reforms on the apparel sector

	Pre-Quota Abolition		Post-Quota Abolition	
	India	Rest of South Asia	India	Rest of South Asia
Output (% change)				
Apparel	25	18	41	53
Exports (% change)				
Apparel	36	16	50	57
Real income $US millions	724	675	2192	1992
% of 2005 GDP	0.16	0.55	0.47	1.6

Source: World Bank staff estimates.

Prior to abolition of the quotas, increase of productivity raises output and exports substantially in the apparel sector of both India and the rest of South Asia. The increase in apparel exports raises textile-sector output in India but reduces it in the rest of South Asia, because in India there is considerable more vertical integration. In all the countries, however, there are significant gains in real incomes. But these gains are constrained by the need to send exports to residual markets, where prices are low to begin with and are further depressed by increased exports.

It is after the abolition of quotas (when India and the rest of South Asia are able to supply additional exports to a much larger market) that the impact of reforms is most beneficial. Thus,

---

[53] The following changes are assumed for India: elimination of the 15 percent export tax equivalent on cotton and cotton based textile; increased total factor productivity (0.2 percent) in the cotton textile sector due to the abolition of the hank yarn obligation; abolition of restrictions on foreign investments and on industry structure in the apparel sector.

productivity-induced increases in exports face a smaller terms-of-trade deterioration, and output and exports rise substantially. The largest change, however, occurs in real income gains flowing from reform. These gains essentially triple in both India and the rest of South Asia when MFA restrictions no longer inhibit exports following increases in competitiveness.

V. IMPACT OF TRADE LIBERALIZATION

An important feature of the projections' baseline is the dramatic reduction in protection in India and the rest of South Asia in the 1990s. To obtain a better understanding of the effect of trade liberalization at the sectoral level, the impact of the reduction in India's[54] tariffs between 1991 and 1998 is examined.[55] Tariff reductions between 1991 and 1998 are presented for each sector together, with the overall impact on volume output and exports (Table 5.6). The tariff reductions are huge, falling by a factor of four. The largest declines in prices of imported goods (and hence import competition) is in apparel, machinery and processed foods, where initial protection rates were especially high.

Clearly, the impact on sectoral output is mixed, with the important, labor-intensive manufacturing sectors, such as apparel and light manufactures, expanding. Other sectors contract, in some cases markedly. The volume of trade, however, expands dramatically, increasing to three times its initial level once the full impact of reform is felt.

Table 5.6. Tariff reductions and their impacts in India

	Tariff 1991	Tariff 1998	Output changes	Export changes
Primary agriculture	47	21	1	89
Processed food	131	35	-0.6	134
Oil and gas	60	25	-55	116
Other energy	73	11	-17	340
Other natural resources	23	12	17	138
Textiles	137	36	-0.4	54
Apparel	130	33	32	91
Light manufactures	96	19	20	365
Heavy manufactures	129	31	-20	345
Machinery and equipment	99	23	-16	925
Utilities, housing, construction	na	na	2	181
Other services	na	na	7	66
Average	84	24	0	201

Source : World Bank staff estimates.

An important feature of the tariff reduction simulation is that exports of textiles and apparel rise by much less than average. This simply reflects the restraining impact of quotas.

---

[54] We analyze only India and not the rest of South Asia because of the availability for India, of tariffs by sector.

[55] Because the MFA quotas will remain in effect until 2005, the analysis was undertaken with these quotas remaining in effect.

While the improved competitiveness of most of India's industries allows a big increase in export volumes, textile and clothing exports to its major markets are unable to expand because of quotas applying in those markets. By contrast, the export tax equivalent increase substantially, which translates into a nine percent fall in the price producers receive for exports to these markets. This disincentive causes exporters to refocus on other sectors, such as transport, machinery and equipment, where exports increase dramatically.

The extraordinary liberalization of the Indian economy is associated with an enormous increase in the importance of trade in the Indian economy, with the share of imports in domestic consumption and the share of exports in total output rising in virtually all sectors (Table 5.6 and 5.7). The increase in imports follows directly from tariff reductions, which reduce production costs and consequently increase competitiveness.

Table 5.7. The impact of liberalization on sectoral import and export shares (percent)

	Import shares		Export shares	
	Initial	Final	Initial	Final
Primary agriculture	1.2	3.2	1.3	2.1
Processed food	2.6	15.9	8.0	18.2
Oil and gas	55.3	88.9	3.8	19.1
Other energy	11.5	34.8	2.7	15.2
Other natural resources	5.7	50.5	27.9	58.0
Textiles	2.1	10.3	7.6	12.5
Apparel	0.4	11.2	35.0	53.6
Light manufactures	5.4	27.5	10.3	40.1
Heavy manufactures	27.2	53.7	6.0	34.0
Machinery and equipment	21.8	68.1	4.6	55.4
Utilities, housing, construction	0.0	0.0	0.0	0.0
Other services	4.3	3.6	2.8	4.9

Source: World Bank staff estimates.

This analysis highlights the profound nature of the transformation under way in the Indian economy as a result of the trade reforms. [If the export orientation of the economy changes to anything like the extent suggested by this analysis, it is clear that radical changes in management practices and production techniques will be required to take advantage of the opportunities created, and to deal with the competitive threat from vastly increased imports.]

CONCLUSIONS

This study has analyzed South Asia's integration in the world economy and discussed future prospects for exports and growth. It concludes that South Asia has made great strides in integrating in the world economy in the past ten years. Trade protection has significantly decreased, financial integration strengthened and export growth in the 1990s has been second only to East Asia. Yet, South Asia remains among the least integrated regions in the world. In regional integration as well, South Asia severely lags behind many other developing-country regions.

Despite India's progress in recent years, growth in South Asia in the 1990's has been slower than in the 1980s, and poverty has not declined significantly. South Asia remains the region with the highest incidence of poverty and the largest number of poor. Sustained progress in poverty reduction critically depends on faster growth, which has been shown to be strongly and positively influenced by integration.

South Asia is now well placed to accelerate integration and growth. Demographic trends will have a positive impact over the next 25 years as the share of the working age population rises.[1] And the combination of a favorable external environment, the implementation of the Uruguay Round, the abolition of the Multi-fibre Arrangement and increased regional cooperation, is potentially formidable and should result in faster growth. Simulating the effects of these factors on South Asia's exports, this study estimated significant gains for South Asia and for India in particular.

Optimism over the buoyant outlook, however, should be tempered for a number of reasons. First, there are no guarantees that the external environment will remain as favorable as predicted. Second, as trade barriers and transport and communications costs fall, competitive pressure will escalate and the world over the next quarter century will be characterized by large shifts in patterns of international specialization. Third, there remains significant constraints that may delay integration. For example, the state of infrastructure is poor and insufficient to meet the needs of an expanding and more outward-oriented economy, because of substantial under-investment and poor maintenance. Despite the progress made in recent years, the state of human development remains low and social indicators are among the worst in developing countries. The cost of financing investments and exports is high, and availability is often limited. Regulations on domestic enterprises (licensing, size entry and exit) and inflexible labor laws impede the realization of economies of scale and are slowing down industrial restructuring. Finally, the continuation of ethnic and civil conflicts may remain the most important factor deterring foreign and domestic investment in some countries.

South Asia will be able to take full advantage of its new opportunities only by stepping up reforms and transforming the role of the state. Increased integration will place new disciplines on government policies, including pressures to sell or close loss-making public enterprises, liberalize labor markets and agricultural exports, and contain fiscal deficits. But it will require

---

[1] See Asian Development Bank (1997).

stronger government intervention in other areas—especially in the financial sector, through a strengthening prudential regulation and effective bank supervision. While this is certainly a demanding agenda, it is necessary in order to reap the benefits of increased international integration in accelerated growth and the eradication of mass poverty.

BIBLIOGRAPHY

Abreu, M. (1996), 'Trade in manufactures: the outcome of the Uruguay Round and developing country interests' in Martin, W. and Winters, L.A. eds *The Uruguay Round and the Developing Countries,* Cambridge University Press, Cambridge.

Ahuja, V. and Filmer, D. (1995), 'Educational attainment in developing countries: new estimates and projections disaggregated by gender: a background paper for the World Development Report 1995', World Bank Working Paper No 1489, World Bank, Washington DC.

Anderson, K., B. Dimaranan, T. Hertel, and W. Martin. "Asia-Pacific Food Markets and Trade in 2005: A Global, Economy-Wide Perspective," Paper Commissioned for the International General Meeting of the Pacific Basin Economic Council Washington, DC, 20-22 May 1996.

Anderson, K. (1990), 'China and the Multifibre Arrangement' in Hamilton, C. *ed. Textiles Trade and the Developing Countries,* World Bank, Washington DC.

Anderson, K. (1983), 'Economic growth, comparative advantage and agricultural trade of Pacific Rim countries' *Review of Marketing and Agricultural Economics* 51(3):231-48.

Bach, C., Martin, W. and Stevens, J. (1996), 'China and the WTO: tariff offers, exemptions, and welfare implications' *Weltwirtschaftliches Archiv* 132(3):409-31.

Ben-David (1993), " Equalizing exchange: trade liberalization and income convergence", Quarterly Journal of Economics, 108, August;

Bhagwati J. (1993), India in transition-Freeing the Economy, Clarendon Press, Oxford.

Balassa, Bela A., (1988), Japan in the World Economy. Institute of International Economics: Washington, D.C.

Bimal, Jalan, (1996), India's Economic Policy, Preparing for the Twenty-First Century. Viking: New Delhi.

Blomström, M., R. Lipsey and M. Zejan (1992), *What Explains the Growth of Developing Countries?*

Borensztein, E., de Gregorio, J. and Lee, Jong-Wha, (1995), "How Does Foreign Direct Investment Affect Growth?" NBER Working Paper 5057. National Bureau of Economic Research, Cambridge, Mass.

Cable, Vincent, (1995), China and India: Economic Reform and Global Integration. Royal Institute of International Affairs: London.

Dasgupta, D., Imai, K. (1997), Technological Development and Foreign Direct Investment, World Bank mimeo.

De Melo, Jaime Panagariya, and Dani Arvind Rodrik, (1993), The New Regionalism: A Country Perspective, Washington, DC: World Bank.

Dollar, D. (1992), "Outward-oriented Developing Economies Really Do Grow More Rapidly: Evidence from 95 LDCs, 1976-1985, Economic Development and Cultural Change.

Dunning, John H. (1994). *Multinational Enterprises and the Global Economy*, Addison-Wesley.

Easterly, W. (1993), "How much do distortions affect growth?" Journal of Monetary Economics,

Elbeher, Hertel, and Martin (1997) *Opportunities and Challenges for South Asia with Abolition of the Multifibre Arrangement*, Washington: World Bank, in process.

Faruqee, Rashid. *Pakistan's Agriculture Sector: Is 3 to 4 percent Annual Growth Sustainable?* Washington: The World Bank, January 1995.

Finger, J. M., Ingco, M. and Reincke, U. (1996), *The Uruguay Round: Statistics on Tariff Concessions Given and Received,* World Bank, Washington DC.

Frankel, J.A. and D.Romer (1995), "Trade and Growth: an empirical investigation", mimeo, UC Berkeley, November.

Hertel, T. *ed.* (1996), *Global Trade Analysis: Modeling and Applications,* Cambridge University Press, New York.

Hertel, T.W., W. Martin, K. Yanagishima, and B. Dimaranan. 1995. "Liberalizing Manufactures Trade in a Changing World Economy," Chapter 4 in W. Martin and L.A. Winters (eds.), *The Uruguay Round and the Developing Economies,* World Bank Discussion Papers No. 307, Washington, DC (also forthcoming Cambridge University Press).

Hertel and others. *Liberalizing Manufactures Trade in a Changing World Economy*, 1995

Hoekman, B. and S. Djankov (1996), " Intra industry Trade, Foreign Direct investment, and the reorientation of eastern European exports", World Bank, PRWP n. 1652.

Husain, Ishrat and Kwang W. Jun, (1993) "Capital Flows to South Asia and ASEAN Countries: Trends, Determinants and Policy Implications," PR Working Paper No. 842, World Bank.

IMF (1995)"India: economic reform and growth" Occasional paper n.134.

International Textiles and Clothing Bureau (1995), 'Proposed Integration by the MFA in the Second and Third Stages', IC/W/96, 22 February 1995.

International Textiles and Clothing Bureau (1996), MFA quotas and quota growth rates, Mimeo, Geneva.

Ingco, Merlinda and Alan Winters (1996), 'Pakistan and the Uruguay Round:Impact and Opportunities,' Background Paper for Pakistan 2010 Report, World Bank, Washington DC, April.

Ingco, M., (1996), 'Tariffication in the Uruguay Round," *The World Economy* 19(4): 425-66.

Kathuria, S. and A. Bhardwaj, "Export and policy constraints in the Indian textiles and garment industry", mimeo, 1997.

Kathuria, S., '*Policy Constraints in the Textiles and garments Industry,*' Mimeo, World Bank, New Delhi, 1997.

Kevin, M., A. Schleifer and R. Vishny. "Industrialization and the Big Push". Journal of Political Economy. 1989. Vol 97, No. 5.

Krishna, K. and Krueger, A. (1995), 'Implementing free trade areas: rules of origin and hidden protection' NBER Working Paper 4983, National Bureau of Economic Research, Cambridge.

Krishna, K., Martin, W. and Tan, L. (forthcoming) 'Imputing license prices: limitations of a cost-based approach' *Journal of Development Studies.*

Kurt Salmon Associates, "Factory cost comparisons study", Dusseldorf, 1995

Martin, W. and Mitra, D. (1996), 'Productivity growth in agriculture and manufacturing', Mimeo, World Bank.

Martin, W. and Winters, A. (1995), The Uruguay Round a Milestone for The Developing Economies, World Bank.

Mukherji Indra N., 1997, "South Asian Preferential Trading Arrangement: identifying products in India's regional trade", mimeo.

Joshi V. and I.M.D. Little (1994), India : Macroeconomics and Political Economy, 1964-1991, World Bank, Washington D.C.

Majd, Nader. *The Uruguay Round and South Asia, An Overview of the Impact and Opportunities*, Policy Research Working Paper No. 1484, Washington: The World Bank, 1995.

National Council of Applied Economic Research (1994), "India: Protection in the consumer goods sector", March, New Dehli, mimeo.

Nerhu, V. and A. Dhareshwar (1994), New estimates of total factor productivity growth for developing and industrial countries, PRWPI, n.1313.

Ng, Francis and Alexander Yeats. (1996), "Open Economies Work Better!" World Bank Policy Research Paper 1636, August.

Pal, R. (1995), "Choppy Waters", Jardine Fleming Securities Limited.

Pritchett, Lant (1991), Measuring Outward Orientation in Developing Countries, Can it Be Done? World Bank Policy, Research and External Affairs Working Paper No. 566. Washington, D.C.

Pursell, G. (1996), "Indian trade policies since the 1991/92 reforms", World Bank mimeo, July.

Raghavan S. N. (1995), "Regional cooperation among SAARC countries", Allied Publishers Limited, New Dehli.

Rogoff, Kenneth (1996), "The Purchasing Power Parity Puzzle." Journal of Economic Literature, June.

Sachs, J., and Warner, A. (1995), "Economic Reform and the Process of Global Integration." *Brookings Papers on Economic Activity* 1. The Brookings Institution.

Selegama, S. (1995), '*NAFTA's impact on the Sri Lankan economy: with special reference to the garment industry*' presented to National Seminar on the Networking of Trade-Related Research Institutions, Colombo, September.

Sengupta N.K., Banik A. and Kathuria R. (1996), "FDI inflows to India in the post reform period: an analysis of the structural and policy impediments", International Management Institute, Occasional Paper.

Summers, Robert and Alan Heston, (1988), "A New Set of International Comparisons of Real Product and Price Levels Estimates for 130 Countries, 1950-1985." Review of Income and Wealth.

Syrquin, Moshe and Hollis B. Chenery, (1989), Patterns of Development, 1950 to 1983. World Bank Discussion Paper 41. Washington, D.C.

Trela, I. and Whalley, J. (1990), 'Global effects of developed country trade restrictions on textiles and apparel' *Economic Journal* 100:1190-1205.

UNCTAD, (1995) World Investment Report: Transnational Corporations and Competitiveness

UNIDO, *Strengthening the Backward Linkages with the Ready-made garment industry*, Bangladesh: United Nations Industrial Development Organization, 1993.

Wacziarg, R. (1997), " Measuring the dynamic gains from trade", IECAP mimeo.

World Bank (1996), "Global Economic Prospects report 1996.

World Bank (1995), "Jobs, Poverty and working conditions in South Asia", Regional perspectives on World Development report 1995.

World Bank (1996), "India : Country Economic Memorandum", August.

World Bank (1997), "India - 1997 Economic Update:Sustaining rapid growth", Report n. 16506-IN

World Bank (1996), "Sri Lanka in the year 2000. An agenda for action", March.

World Bank (1997), "India- Cotton and Textile Industries: Maximizing the Potential for Growth in a more competitive environment", March, Report n. 16347-IN.

World Trade Organization (1994), *The Results of the Uruguay Round of Multilateral Trade Negotiations: The Legal Texts*, World Trade Organization, Geneva.

Yang, Y., Martin, W. and Yanagishima, Y. (1997), 'Evaluating the benefits of abolishing the MFA in the Uruguay Round package' in Hertel, T. ed. *Global Trade Analysis: Using the GTAP Model*, Cambridge University Press, New York.

ANNEXES

ANNEXES

ANNEX I.I

TRADE INDICATORS .

Table I.1 South Asia: basic economic indicators

	Population, 1996		GNP, 1996		GNP per Capita, 1996 (US$)	Real GDP Growth (%) (based on 1987 constant US$)			Real GDP per Capita Growth Rate (%)	
	(Million)	(%)	(Billion US$)	(%)		1981-1990	1991-1995	1996	1991-95	1996
Bangladesh	122	9.8	32.4	7.1	266	4.7	4.1	4.4	2.4	2.5
India	946	76.2	341.6	75.0	361	5.8	4.4	6.8	2.5	4.9
Nepal	22	1.8	4.3	0.9	197	4.7	5.1	5.3	2.5	2.7
Pakistan	134	10.8	63.2	13.9	474	6.3	4.7	5.9	1.7	0.3
Sri Lanka	18	1.5	14.2	3.1	775	4.4	4.5	5.8	3.1	4.7
South Asia	1242	100	455.8	100	367	5.8	4.4	6.5	2.5	4.6

Note: * This number may be updated in light of further research.
Source: IEC, World Bank

Table I.2 Structural changes in labor force

	Agriculture		Industry		Services	
	1965	1986-89	1965	1989-92	1965	1986-89
BANGLADESH	84	56	5	10	11	34
INDIA	73	63	12	11	15	27
NEPAL	94	93	2	1	4	6
PAKISTAN	60	50	18	12	22	38
SRI LANKA	56	43	14	12	30	46

Source: S.N.Raghavan (1995)

Table I.3 Structure of merchandise imports, selected years

Country		(Unit: %) Energy	Food	Other Consumer Goods	Capital Goods	Intermediate Goods			Total	Averaged Annual Growth	
							Manufactur	Primary		1986-1990	1991-1995
BANGLADESH	1985	14	23	26	26	12	n.a.	n.a.	100	10	18
	1994	7	7	43	32	11	2	9	100		
INDIA	1985	23	8	10	20	38	26	12	100	11	14
	1994	17	4	7	23	50	31	19	100		
NEPAL	1985	11	11	0	58	20	n.a.	n.a.	100	11	16
	1994	10	13	0	56	20	n.a.	n.a.	100		
PAKISTAN	1985	17	18	17	27	21	14	6	100	8	8
	1994	17	12	16	36	19	12	7	100		
SRI LANKA	1985	21	11	9	20	48	n.a.	n.a.	100	10	14
	1994	6	12	9	28	44	44	0	100		

Source: IEC, World Bank

Table I.4 Structure of demand as share of GDP, 1980-1995 (percent)

Country	Total consumption 1980	1990	1994	1995	Gross domestic investment 1980	1990	1994	1995	Gross domestic savings 1980	1990	1994	1995	Exports of GNFS 1980	1990	1994	1995	Resource balance 1980	1990	1994	1995
Banglades	97.9	97.3	90.9	93.3	14.9	12.8	15.4	15.0	2.1	2.7	9.1	6.7	5.7	8.5	11.9	14.2	-12.8	-10.1	-6.4	-8.3
Bhutan	92.1	91.0	89.3	n.a.	31.0	20.3	32.2	n.a.	7.9	9.0	10.7	n.a.	13.1	32.5	31.4	n.a.	-23.1	-11.3	-21.6	n.a.
India	82.6	77.6	78.5	77.3	20.9	25.2	23.2	24.4	17.4	22.4	21.5	22.7	6.5	7.7	11.3	12.4	-3.5	-2.8	-1.7	-1.6
Maldives	95.4	74.8	n.a.	n.a.	44.2*	83.5*	n.a.	n.a.	4.6	25.2	n.a.	n.a.	18.2	36.1	n.a.	n.a.	-39.6	-58.3	n.a.	n.a.
Nepal	88.9	92.1	87.6	n.a.	18.3	18.4	20.5	n.a.	11.1	7.9	12.4	n.a.	11.5	10.5	23.9	n.a.	-7.2	-10.6	-8.1	n.a.
Pakistan	93.1	86.5	83.2	83.3*	18.5	18.9	19.5	19.1	6.9	13.5	16.8	16.7	12.5	14.8	16.2	16.2	-11.6	-5.5	-2.8	-2.4
Sri Lanka	88.8	84.5	85.0	85.6	33.8	21.9	27.0	25.9	11.2	14.1	15.0	14.4	32.2	29.8	33.7	33.6	-22.6	-7.8	-11.9	-11.4

Note: * Figures are calculated as residual from other GDP components.
Source: IEC. World Bank

Table I.5 Structure of merchandise exports, selected years

		Total Manufactures	Total Primaries	Food	Total Merchandise
WORLD	1985	63.1	36.9	10.2	100
	1994	76.7	23.3	9.1	100
BANGLADESH	1985	66.0	34.0	20.0	100
	1994	86.0	14.0	11.6	100
INDIA	1985	54.3	45.7	19.7	100
	1994	75.9	23.9	15.5	100
NEPAL	1985	75.1	23.5	18.9	100
	1994	93.5	6.5	5.0	100
PAKISTAN	1985	60.7	39.3	16.2	100
	1994	87.2	12.5	8.1	100
SRI LANKA	1985	42.2	56.8	43.7	100
	1994	78.2	21.7	16.7	100

Source: United Nations, TARS (World Bank)

Table I.6 Share of Differentiated and Science-based Goods in Manufacturing Exports (%)

	1970	1975	1980	1985	1990	1995
Bangladesh	..	..	1.2	0.8	1.0	..
India	4.0	5.6	7.4	6.7	9.2	7.7 *
Nepal	..	0.0	0.0	0.1	0.2	0.2
Pakistan	1.7	2.6	1.7	2.6	2.0	2.0
Sri Lanka	0.2	0.5	0.7	1.0	2.4	3.4
China					15.4	23.2
Hong Kong	14.9	19.5	29.6	31.4	35.8	37.8
Indonesia	0.5	0.7	0.7	1.2	2.3	9.0
Korea	8.8	13.5	16.9	19.6	32.5	42.6
Malaysia	1.6	9.9	12.1	18.7	36.2	56.8
Philippines	0.2	0.9	2.9	7.6	13.1	22.3
Singapore	9.4	23.0	25.8	34.3	52.0	68.5
Thailand	0.4	1.8	6.5	9.8	23.1	35.4
Brazil	3.7	7.3	10.6	9.3	12.1	12.8
Canada	13.6	12.9	12.1	11.5	16.5	17.8
France	26.1	27.5	26.2	29.2	31.5	35.1
Germany	36.5	35.7	33.6	32.8	36.2	37.7
Italy	30.5	27.9	27.3	28.4	31.9	32.6
Japan	28.7	27.6	36.4	44.4	50.3	54.2
USA	42.2	43.5	42.2	45.9	45.7	46.8

Note: * based on 1994
Source: IEC, World Bank

Table I.7 Nominal merchandise export and import growth, 1981-1996

	Import Growth (%)			Export Growth (%)			Export to Import Ratio (%)		
	1981-90	1991-95	1996	1981-90	1991-95	1996	1980	1990	1996
World	5.9	7.7	5.2	5.8	8.0	4.5	102.6	101.9	102.3
South Asia	5.3	8.5	5.9	8.0	12.5	6.7	49.7	64.1	77.2
Bangladesh	4.8	9.0	23.4	7.8	17.9	15.0	30.5	40.2	55.5
India	5.8	8.3	5.0	8.3	12.2	6.1	52.4	66.2	79.7
Nepal	8.5	15.4	13.4	6.5	14.8	0.8	33.9	28.2	24.3
Pakistan	4.3	6.5	-0.4	7.7	10.4	9.6	48.2	66.5	87.6
Sri Lanka	2.3	13.8	3.5	5.7	15.4	-1.4	57.5	79.7	81.4

Source: IEC, World Bank

Annex I.I Trade indicators

Table I.8 Contribution of quantity and prices to export growth, 1986-90 and 1991-95
(Current US$, merchandise exports)

| | | Annual Average Growth Rate (%) | | | |
		Value	Quantity	Price	Residual
Bangladesh	1986-1990	10.3	9.7	0.5	0.0
	1991-1995	17.9	17.6	0.3	0.0
	1991	12.7	14.0	-1.1	-0.2
	1992	16.0	14.8	1.1	0.2
	1993	19.6	22.3	-2.3	-0.5
	1994	6.4	5.7	0.6	0.0
	1995	37.0	33.1	2.9	1.0
	1996	15.0	10.1	4.5	0.5
India	1986-1990	14.3	9.8	4.1	0.4
	1991-1995	12.2	12.0	0.2	0.0
	1991	-1.1	-0.1	-1.0	0.0
	1992	3.3	9.6	-5.7	-0.6
	1993	20.2	21.4	-1.0	-0.2
	1994	18.4	14.0	3.9	0.5
	1995	22.1	16.3	5.0	0.8
	1996	6.1	8.2	-2.0	-0.2
Nepal	1986-1990	3.2	0.8	2.4	0.0
	1991-1995	14.8	11.7	2.7	0.3
	1991	26.1	22.2	3.2	0.7
	1992	41.2	37.6	2.7	1.0
	1993	18.3	18.0	0.2	0.0
	1994	3.8	-0.2	4.1	0.0
	1995	-9.0	-12.0	3.5	-0.4
	1996	0.8	-2.2	3.1	-0.1
Pakistan	1986-1990	14.9	8.2	6.2	0.5
	1991-1995	10.4	8.5	1.8	0.1
	1991	19.8	21.1	-1.1	-0.2
	1992	14.6	17.1	-2.2	-0.4
	1993	0.3	2.0	-1.7	0.0
	1994	-0.5	1.6	-2.1	0.0
	1995	19.7	2.1	17.2	0.4
	1996	9.6	-1.5	11.3	-0.2
Sri Lanka	1986-1990	7.1	5.0	2.0	0.1
	1991-1995	15.4	14.5	0.9	0.1
	1991	8.1	10.5	-2.1	-0.2
	1992	14.9	20.2	-4.4	-0.9
	1993	21.0	22.4	-1.1	-0.2
	1994	14.9	12.0	2.6	0.3
	1995	18.7	7.9	9.9	0.8
	1996	-1.4	5.7	-6.8	-0.4

Source: Staff Estimation based on database of IEC, World Bank

Table I.9 Direction of exports, 1986 and 1995

	USA 1986	USA 1995	EU15 1986	EU15 1995	JAPAN 1986	JAPAN 1995	EAST ASIA 1986	EAST ASIA 1995	REST OF THE 1986	REST OF THE 1995	WORLD 1986	WORLD 1995
BANGLADESH	32.23	35.98	29.78	46.31	10.09	3.90	6.62	6.48	21.29	7.33	100	100
INDIA	27.73	20.69	27.82	35.60	14.60	9.93	8.65	21.24	21.20	12.55	100	100
NEPAL	23.19	33.14	28.46	59.25	0.99	0.54	3.77	1.15	43.58	5.92	100	100
PAKISTAN	12.35	17.93	37.21	37.98	12.32	8.33	12.76	24.31	25.36	11.44	100	100
SRI LANKA	30.40	38.44	30.14	37.69	7.21	6.68	6.17	6.82	26.07	10.37	100	100
SOUTH ASIA	25.03	23.03	30.07	37.24	13.05	8.83	9.09	19.19	22.75	11.70	100	100

Source: United Nations, TARS (World Bank)

Table I.10 Direction of imports, 1986 and 1995

	USA 1986	USA 1995	EU15 1986	EU15 1995	JAPAN 1986	JAPAN 1995	EAST ASIA 1986	EAST ASIA 1995	REST OF THE WORLD 1986	REST OF THE WORLD 1995	WORLD 1986	WORLD 1995
BANGLADESH	8.08	7.26	17.28	14.44	22.43	7.83	33.82	56.69	18.39	13.79	100	100
INDIA	11.39	11.32	45.27	43.94	15.91	9.12	12.01	21.08	15.42	14.55	100	100
NEPAL	2.77	1.88	14.91	12.89	23.81	11.62	23.14	60.46	35.37	13.15	100	100
PAKISTAN	15.54	10.82	35.46	31.70	19.14	14.37	15.25	31.60	14.60	11.51	100	100
SRI LANKA	4.62	6.86	23.95	23.46	20.63	10.83	33.70	46.42	17.10	12.43	100	100
SOUTH ASIA	11.44	10.33	38.78	36.59	17.63	10.16	16.27	29.22	15.87	13.70	100	100

Source: United Nations, TARS (World Bank)

Table I.11 Partner contribution to nominal export growth (%)

	USA 1981-9	USA 1991-9	EU15 1981-9	EU15 1991-9	EAST ASIA 1981-9	EAST ASIA 1991-9	JAPAN 1981-9	JAPAN 1991-9	REST OF THE WORLD 1981-90	REST OF THE WORLD 1991-94	TOTAL 1981-9	TOTAL 1991-94
BANGLADES	5.46	6.72	2.71	8.14	0.55	1.09	0.95	0.16	3.48	-0.74	13.15	15.37
INDIA	2.67	2.72	2.93	2.97	1.75	3.33	1.08	0.68	1.93	1.33	10.35	11.02
NEPAL	5.40	5.49	9.87	6.94	0.18	-0.78	-1.09	0.03	8.55	3.04	22.91	14.72
PAKISTAN	1.95	1.88	4.38	1.92	1.87	2.65	1.49	0.11	2.27	-0.11	11.96	6.45
SRI LANKA	3.88	6.37	1.98	5.53	0.98	0.76	0.68	0.55	2.67	-1.40	10.18	11.81
SOUTH ASIA	2.84	3.13	3.04	3.34	1.59	2.74	1.05	0.51	2.04	0.73	10.56	10.44

Source: United Nations, TARS (World Bank)

Table I.12 Partner contribution to nominal import growth (%)

	USA 1981-90	USA 1991-94	EU15 1981-9	EU15 1991-9	EAST ASIA 1981-90	EAST ASIA 1991-9	JAPAN 1981-9	JAPAN 1991-9	REST OF THE WORL 1981-90	REST OF THE WORL 1991-94	TOTAL 1981-90	TOTAL 1991-94
BANGLADES	-0.18	0.46	0.14	0.29	3.72	6.22	0.20	-0.39	1.71	3.57	5.58	10.14
INDIA	0.44	-0.12	3.86	0.96	1.26	3.17	0.88	0.45	1.55	1.82	7.99	6.28
NEPAL	0.49	-0.15	2.18	-0.92	4.51	5.67	1.33	0.64	2.14	4.84	10.66	10.08
PAKISTAN	0.99	-1.54	1.24	2.44	1.84	4.12	0.97	-0.19	-0.19	-0.23	4.85	4.60
SRI LANKA	0.48	0.62	0.25	4.81	3.35	6.86	0.47	1.27	-0.36	5.53	4.19	19.08
SOUTH ASIA	0.46	-0.39	2.54	1.41	1.77	3.96	0.77	0.24	0.95	1.81	6.48	7.03

Source: United Nations, TARS (World Bank)

Table I.13 Market share in import markets and import growth; 1980-1994

| | Market Share (%) | | | | Average Growth (%) | |
	1980	1985	1990	1994	80-90	91-94
US Import	100	100	100	100	7.42	10.63
from						
BANGLADESH	0.040	0.063	0.115	0.168	19.47	26.61
INDIA	0.478	0.685	0.661	0.822	10.96	18.26
NEPAL	0.002	0.015	0.012	0.020	25.46	27.13
PAKISTAN	0.055	0.083	0.127	0.157	16.68	15.01
SRI LANKA	0.055	0.087	0.112	0.170	15.30	21.51
South Asia	0.631	0.932	1.027	1.338	12.78	19.30
EU15 Import	100	100	100	100	6.18	0.29
from						
BANGLADESH	0.040	0.032	0.044	0.086	7.35	16.83
INDIA	0.309	0.328	0.396	0.543	8.84	11.62
NEPAL	0.002	0.005	0.009	0.013	21.84	8.17
PAKISTAN	0.081	0.105	0.130	0.153	11.35	5.13
SRI LANKA	0.041	0.046	0.043	0.073	6.75	13.61
South Asia	0.472	0.518	0.622	0.867	9.14	10.91
East Asia Import	100	100	100	100	13.00	19.94
from						
BANGLADESH	0.035	0.033	0.023	0.024	8.44	19.72
INDIA	0.497	0.482	0.636	0.672	15.83	15.18
NEPAL	0.005	0.003	0.004	0.001	9.57	-13.31
PAKISTAN	0.265	0.192	0.236	0.192	11.71	7.49
SRI LANKA	0.043	0.067	0.032	0.026	9.72	9.31
South Asia	0.845	0.777	0.931	0.916	14.11	13.28
Japan Import	100	100	100	100	5.27	5.09
from						
BANGLADESH	0.020	0.065	0.030	0.033	9.73	10.75
INDIA	0.722	0.918	0.884	0.970	7.42	6.76
NEPAL	0.006	0.001	0.001	0.001	-11.25	24.03
PAKISTAN	0.151	0.295	0.229	0.200	9.75	-5.39
SRI LANKA	0.039	0.061	0.057	0.069	9.34	12.77
South Asia	0.937	1.339	1.201	1.273	7.90	4.79
Rest of World Imp	100	100	100	100	7.55	8.55
from						
BANGLADESH	0.029	0.057	0.049	0.031	13.32	1.17
INDIA	0.392	0.470	0.494	0.488	10.06	3.31
NEPAL	0.009	0.013	0.005	0.008	1.89	8.72
PAKISTAN	0.139	0.145	0.159	0.119	9.01	-2.89
SRI LANKA	0.064	0.088	0.078	0.047	9.75	-1.37
South Asia	0.633	0.772	0.785	0.694	9.90	1.76

Source: United Nations, TARS (World Bank)

Table I.14 Real GDP, export volume, world demand, and real effective exchange rate (1987 constant US$, merchandise exports)

Bangladesh	Real GDP	Export Volume	World Demand	Real Effective Exchange rate
1979	62.4	46.0	58.7	124.7
1980	63.3	53.0	59.8	111.7
1981	69.3	54.2	58.0	111.5
1982	71.9	47.9	57.6	106.1
1983	75.2	53.0	59.0	105.1
1984	78.8	58.5	64.7	116.6
1985	81.9	62.8	67.8	119.6
1986	85.5	64.3	75.3	103.9
1987	89.0	78.2	80.4	100.2
1988	91.5	84.5	88.1	99.8
1989	93.8	88.6	93.9	106.7
1990	100	100	100	100
1991	103.4	114.0	105.4	98.2
1992	107.7	130.8	110.4	92.3
1993	112.4	160.0	110.9	91.6
1994	117.1	169.1	121.8	88.3
1995	122.2	225.0	131.3	86.0
1996	127.6	247.8	136.2	85.7

India	Real GDP	Export Volume	World Demand	Real Effective Exchange rate
1979	53.1	62.6	59.3	155.5
1980	56.7	57.4	62.1	172.8
1981	60.4	54.8	59.0	179.2
1982	62.7	56.0	58.9	172.7
1983	67.3	58.5	62.1	177.7
1984	69.8	61.3	64.9	176.9
1985	73.6	62.7	74.3	170.8
1986	77.1	67.3	77.3	145.9
1987	80.8	75.8	80.0	132.3
1988	88.8	80.3	88.9	122.8
1989	94.7	95.5	92.2	111.0
1990	100	100	100	100
1991	100.5	99.9	89.1	85.2
1992	105.8	109.4	96.7	71.9
1993	110.0	132.8	111.4	71.4
1994	116.9	151.4	137.3	73.9
1995	124.1	176.0	166.0	71.3
1996	132.5	190.5	169.8	70.0

Nepal	Real GDP	Export Volume	World Demand	Real Effective Exchange rate
1979	64.5	53.0	63.6	120.6
1980	63.0	50.0	64.0	120.0
1981	68.3	74.1	61.3	127.3
1982	70.8	72.4	60.8	139.0
1983	68.7	50.7	62.9	141.3
1984	75.4	67.3	68.2	130.8
1985	80.0	96.1	73.1	129.3
1986	83.6	88.5	80.9	115.1
1987	85.0	73.9	83.0	113.4
1988	91.6	101.1	89.1	109.8
1989	95.5	94.6	94.1	106.1
1990	100	100	100	100
1991	106.3	122.2	101.7	90.5
1992	110.5	168.1	106.7	88.6
1993	114.7	198.4	108.8	84.3
1994	124.1	197.9	120.0	84.6
1995	128.2	174.1	128.6	79.7
1996	135.0	170.2	134.6	80.6

Pakistan	Real GDP	Export Volume	World Demand	Real Effective Exchange rate
1979	49.2	41.3	56.1	197.5
1980	54.4	51.9	59.0	166.9
1981	58.7	62.7	60.0	188.7
1982	62.5	57.0	60.2	173.0
1983	66.7	64.4	61.5	166.9
1984	70.2	67.7	66.6	170.0
1985	75.5	67.5	68.9	158.8
1986	79.6	82.0	73.8	131.1
1987	84.7	85.4	79.5	116.0
1988	91.3	95.7	87.5	114.0
1989	95.7	100.5	94.1	106.9
1990	100	100	100	100
1991	105.5	121.1	104.7	98.1
1992	113.7	141.9	110.9	96.8
1993	115.9	144.8	115.5	96.5
1994	120.4	147.1	125.4	94.3
1995	125.7	150.2	138.0	93.6
1996	133.1	147.9	145.5	91.8

Sri Lanka	Real GDP	Export Volume	World Demand	Real Effective Exchange rate
1979	61.3	55.8	90.2	98.8
1980	64.8	54.7	101.3	113.6
1981	68.5	59.2	91.7	120.8
1982	73.6	59.8	103.6	128.2
1983	77.2	57.7	105.0	127.5
1984	80.9	70.1	106.9	141.9
1985	85.0	78.5	115.9	132.6
1986	88.6	75.6	113.8	118.0
1987	89.7	81.3	111.4	105.6
1988	92.1	85.1	104.9	104.8
1989	94.1	87.8	101.0	99.5
1990	100	100	100	100
1991	100.7	110.5	120.0	104.8
1992	104.7	132.8	125.0	104.5
1993	111.9	162.5	149.3	106.2
1994	118.1	182.0	167.6	106.5
1995	124.4	196.5	171.2	101.4
1996	131.6	207.7	173.9	110.2

Source: IEC, World Bank

Annex 1.1 Trade indicators

Table I.15 Trade policy indicators, early 1990s

| | Tariff-Unweighted average (%) | | Non-tariff measures--coverage (%) | |
	Primary	Manufactures	Primary	Manufactures
South Asia				
India	45	56	72	59
Pakistan	54	64	7	17
Bangladesh	73	85	55	47
Sri Lanka	27	26	3	4
Nepal	9	19	1	1
Large Countries				
Brazil	7	16	4	0
China	32	40	12	11
Indonesia	14	18	5	2
Nigeria	29	34	23	3
East Asia				
Korea	13	11	9	0
Malaysia	7	15	1	2
Taiwan, China	6	11	58	29
Thailand	26	42	9	4

Source: Ng and Yeats (1996)

Table I.16 Structure of production (percent share of GDP)

| | Agriculture | | | Industry | | | Manufacturing | | | Services, etc. | | |
	1970	1980	93-95	1970	1980	93-95	1970	1980	93-95	1970	1980	93-95
Bangladesh	55	50	30	9	16	18	6	11	10	37	34	52
India	45	38	30	22	26	28	15	18	18	33	36	41
Nepal	67	62	43	12	12	22	4	4	9	21	26	35
Pakistan	37	30	25	22	25	25	16	16	17	41	46	50
Sri Lanka	28	28	24	24	30	25	17	18	15	48	43	52
South Asia	41	39	28	19	24	25	13	15	16	32	34	40
East Asia & Pacific	31	27	18	31	39	44	23	27	31	28	32	39
[Europe & Central Asia	..	..	12	..	..	35	..	..	..	..	..	44
Latin America & Caribbean	12	10	10	34	37	32	23	25	20	51	51	55
Middle East & North Africa	..	8	12	..	57	..	..	7	10	..	32	..
Sub-Saharan Africa	25	24	19	26	36	28	12	12	15	43	38	47
High income	..	3	2	..	37	32	..	24	21	..	57	66
Low & middle income	..	16	14	..	..	35	..	..	20	..	..	47
World	..	7	5	..	38	33	..	23	21	..	53	63

Source: World Development Indicator 1997, World Bank

Table I.17 Performance of key export sectors, 1980-1995

BANGLADESH

	Annual Averaged Growth Rate (%)						Share (%)				
	1980-85	1985-90	1990-95	1980-90	1985-95	1985-94*	1980	1985	1990	1994	1995
Agriculture and allied	12.4	4.3	5.7	8.3	5.0	5.3	24.5	31.6	18.4	13.6	11.2
Textiles and garments	14.2	21.6	20.3	17.9	21.0	20.2	37.6	52.7	66.0	74.6	77.2
Gems and jewelry	1.3	21.3	-0.1	10.9	10.1	5.6	0.0	0.0	0.0	0.0	0.0
Chemicals	20.7	30.4	18.5	25.5	24.3	18.9	0.6	1.1	1.9	1.4	2.1
Engineering goods (excl. auto parts)	-48.9	13.0	17.8	-24.0	15.4	31.0	21.3	0.5	0.5	1.6	0.5
Auto parts	17.3	13.5	58.1	15.4	34.0	8.2	0.0	0.0	0.0	0.0	0.1
Leathers, total	14.2	18.5	3.0	16.3	10.5	9.2	6.8	9.4	10.4	5.6	5.6
Others	-6.8	5.3	20.4	-1.0	12.6	10.7	9.2	4.7	2.8	3.2	3.3
Total	6.8	16.3	16.6	11.4	16.4	15.7	100	100	100	100.0	100
(Memo items)											
FOOTWEAR	9.2	91.4	73.3	44.6	82.1	92.3	0.0	0.0	0.1	0.7	0.7
TRAVEL GOODS,HANDBAGS	-10.9	13.6	45.7	0.6	28.6	33.0	0.2	0.1	0.1	0.2	0.2

INDIA

	Annual Averaged Growth Rate (%)						Share (%)				
	1980-85	1985-90	1990-95	1980-90	1985-95	1985-94	1980	1985	1990	1994	1995
Agriculture and allied	2.1	9.5	7.4	5.7	8.5	9.4	29.3	24.7	19.7	18.5	16.2
Textiles and garments	-0.3	21.6	13.3	10.1	17.3	17.6	27.5	20.6	27.8	29.8	29.8
Gems and jewelry	10.4	24.4	9.7	17.2	16.8	16.9	10.8	13.5	20.3	18.3	18.6
Chemicals	6.5	31.6	23.1	18.4	27.3	26.1	2.1	2.2	4.4	5.9	7.1
Engineering goods (excl. auto parts)	1.6	13.1	14.6	7.2	13.9	12.8	8.4	6.9	6.5	6.8	7.4
Auto parts	-4.1	25.9	17.5	9.9	21.7	21.6	1.4	0.8	1.4	1.6	1.8
Leathers, total	6.0	11.2	3.9	8.6	7.5	7.2	4.6	4.7	4.1	2.9	2.8
Others	17.0	3.5	11.9	10.0	7.6	6.8	16.0	26.6	16.0	16.0	16.2
Total	5.6	14.6	11.6	10.0	13.1	12.9	100	100	100	100.0	100
(Memo items)											
FOOTWEAR	5.0	19.9	10.9	12.2	15.3	16.0	0.9	0.9	1.1	1.2	1.1
TRAVEL GOODS,HANDBAGS	9.3	26.5	17.7	17.6	22.0	22.5	0.5	0.6	1.0	1.2	1.3

NEPAL

	Annual Averaged Growth Rate (%)						Share (%)				
	1980-85	1985-90	1990-95	1980-90	1985-95	1985-94	1980	1985	1990	1994	1995
Agriculture and allied	0.3	-10.8	-23.7	-5.4	-17.5	-2.6	50.0	23.3	7.8	6.4	1.5
Textiles and garments	42.6	19.3	7.8	30.4	13.4	17.4	21.5	58.0	83.0	85.9	90.6
Gems and jewelry	0.2	50.5	7.4	22.8	27.1	28.5	0.4	0.2	0.9	0.6	0.9
Chemicals	8.4	-27.5	-24.9	-11.3	-26.2	-3.6	5.7	3.9	0.5	1.0	0.1
Engineering goods (excl. auto parts)	31.7	-2.3	3.0	13.4	0.3	-2.9	2.5	4.5	2.3	1.2	2.0
Auto parts	113.4	-11.2	16.7	37.7	1.8	17.8	0.0	0.1	0.0	0.1	0.1
Leathers, total	-2.4	-3.9	0.2	-3.2	-1.9	-6.0	14.8	6.0	2.9	1.2	2.2
Others	10.9	1.7	6.4	6.2	4.0	10.6	5.2	4.0	2.6	3.5	2.6
Total	16.8	11.1	6.0	13.9	8.5	12.4	100	100	100	100.0	100
(Memo items)											
FOOTWEAR	-16.8	1.5	10.1	-8.1	5.7	32.9	0.0	0.0	0.0	0.0	0.0
TRAVEL GOODS,HANDBAGS	-14.0	58.2	35.2	16.6	46.2	60.7	0.1	0.0	0.2	0.7	0.6

PAKISTAN

	Annual Averaged Growth Rate (%)						Share (%)				
	1980-85	1985-90	1990-95	1980-90	1985-95	1985-94	1980	1985	1990	1994	1995
Agriculture and allied	5.6	5.9	-7.2	5.8	-0.9	-1.7	37.8	37.3	22.8	11.5	11.0
Textiles and garments	4.5	26.1	12.2	14.8	18.9	19.5	45.2	42.3	61.7	75.5	77.2
Gems and jewelry	14.2	16.0	-1.8	15.1	6.7	7.5	0.3	0.4	0.4	0.3	0.3
Chemicals	44.3	-18.1	0.3	8.7	-9.4	-10.3	0.7	3.1	0.5	0.4	0.4
Engineering goods (excl. auto parts)	9.9	3.5	5.6	6.7	4.5	3.4	1.8	2.1	1.2	1.0	1.1
Auto parts	-25.9	91.0	-9.2	19.0	31.7	19.2	0.1	0.0	0.1	0.0	0.0
Leathers, total	17.2	13.5	-0.6	15.3	6.2	6.0	4.2	7.1	6.1	4.3	4.1
Others	0.6	15.4	3.1	7.7	9.1	10.6	10.0	7.7	7.3	6.9	6.0
Total	5.9	16.9	7.3	11.3	12.0	12.0	100	100	100	100.0	100
(Memo items)											
FOOTWEAR	-0.4	9.9	13.0	4.6	11.4	8.6	0.7	0.5	0.4	0.4	0.5
TRAVEL GOODS,HANDBAGS	12.1	34.5	5.9	22.8	19.3	21.0	0.1	0.2	0.3	0.3	0.3

SRI LANKA

	Annual Averaged Growth Rate (%)						Share (%)				
	1980-85	1985-90	1990-95	1980-90	1985-95	1985-94	1980	1985	1990	1994	1995
Agriculture and allied	5.0	3.3	-1.1	4.1	1.1	0.3	61.9	52.3	36.4	20.4	19.6
Textiles and garments	20.9	18.7	19.6	19.8	19.1	19.7	16.8	28.7	40.0	55.3	55.5
Gems and jewelry	-3.8	35.9	4.2	14.3	19.0	18.8	6.9	3.8	10.4	6.7	7.2
Chemicals	18.1	10.5	11.2	14.3	10.9	11.2	0.6	0.9	0.9	0.9	0.8
Engineering goods (excl. auto parts)	22.7	0.1	19.9	10.8	9.6	8.5	2.6	4.7	2.8	3.8	4.0
Auto parts	4.6	-2.7	60.1	0.9	24.8	29.7	0.0	0.0	0.0	0.1	0.1
Leathers, total	-12.5	9.0	-12.6	-2.4	-2.4	0.5	0.4	0.1	0.1	0.1	0.0
Others	5.7	10.9	19.2	8.3	15.0	15.2	10.7	9.4	9.3	12.7	12.7
Total	8.6	11.0	12.0	9.8	11.5	11.3	100	100	100	100.0	100
(Memo items)											
FOOTWEAR	51.5	26.0	24.9	38.1	25.4	28.9	0.1	0.4	0.7	1.4	1.2
TRAVEL GOODS,HANDBAGS	20.6	68.1	67.9	42.4	68.0	69.7	0.0	0.0	0.2	1.3	1.8

SOUTH ASIA 5

	Annual Averaged Growth Rate (%)						Share (%)				
	1980-85	1985-90	1990-95	1980-90	1985-95	1985-94	1980	1985	1990	1994	1995
Agriculture and allied	3.8	7.4	3.8	5.6	5.6	6.0	33.2	29.8	21.4	17.0	15.1
Textiles and garments	4.1	22.6	14.3	12.9	18.4	18.7	30.4	27.6	38.4	43.5	44.0
Gems and jewelry	9.6	24.9	9.4	17.0	16.9	16.9	7.9	9.3	14.2	12.8	13.0
Chemicals	12.2	23.5	22.2	17.7	22.8	21.3	1.7	2.2	3.2	4.2	5.1
Engineering goods (excl. auto parts)	-0.5	11.6	14.5	5.4	13.0	12.2	7.5	5.4	4.7	5.2	5.5
Auto parts	-4.1	26.2	17.4	10.0	21.7	21.6	0.9	0.6	0.9	1.1	1.2
Leathers, total	8.9	12.6	2.6	10.7	7.5	7.1	4.4	5.0	4.6	3.1	3.0
Others	14.0	4.9	11.7	9.3	8.2	7.6	14.0	20.1	12.8	13.1	13.1
Total	6.1	14.8	11.2	10.3	13.0	12.8	100.0	100.0	100.0	100.0	100.0
(Memo items)											
FOOTWEAR	5.1	19.3	13.3	12.0	16.3	17.0	0.8	0.7	0.9	1.0	1.0
TRAVEL GOODS,HANDBAGS	9.1	27.5	20.0	18.0	23.7	24.1	0.4	0.4	0.7	1.0	1.0

Source: United Nations, TARS (World Bank)

ANNEX I.II

ADJUSTING THE TRADE TO GDP RATIOS

Chapter I discussed the level of openness and changes in the nominal level of trade to GDP ratios in South Asia and other countries. But how can we interpret these results? Unfortunately, their interpretation is not straightforward. They are influenced not only by policies but a variety of structural factors and endowments. Table I.18 presents the results of adjusting trade to GDP ratios for structural characteristics.

Table I.18 Adjusted trade to GDP ratios, 1975-79 to 1990-94

Region or group	Real growth[a] differential (% Points)	Adjusted[b] 1990-94 %	PPP adjusted[c] 1990-94 %
World	0.7		
OECD	0.8		
USA	0.6	27.1	28.2
Japan	0.2	40.8	46.2
Developing Countries	0.3		
East Asia	1.3		
China	1.2	19.8	20.1
Korea	1.5	52.8	59.1
South Asia	0.2		
India	0.2	21.4	24.6
Pakistan	-0.2	33.4	36.7
Bangladesh	0.3	40.1	44.5
Sri Lanka	0.4	58.9	60.5
Nepal	0.1	49.8	n.a.
Latin America	0.7		
Brazil	0.4	27.3	26.7
Low-Income Countries	-0.8		
Large Developing Countries	-0.4		.
Exporters of manufactures	2.2		

a. Annual average change in ratios of trade to GDP, both in constant price terms.
b. Trade ratios adjusted for factor endowments and income.
c. Trade to PPP GDP adjusted for factor endowments and income
Source: World Bank.

Trade to GDP ratios measured in nominal terms are highly sensitive to movements in real exchange rates. Depreciation would increase the ratio by increasing prices of exports and imports relative to the GDP price deflator. In Japan and Korea, trade ratios have fallen in the past 10 years as exchange rates appreciated. It would be hard however, to conclude that these two countries became less integrated with the world economy. Japan, for example, relocated part of its production offshore and expanded outward foreign investment. Similarly, depreciation of China's currency in the past decade contributed to an increase in the trade ratio (which was also influenced by trade reforms and liberalization of foreign investments.) The depreciation of currencies of South Asian countries in the 1990s contributed to the moderate rise in their trade openness ratio. In constant price terms, South Asia's real annual change in trade openness is 0.2 percent, much lower than the nominal annual change of 0.5 percent. It is lower than in East Asia (1.3 percent), Latin America (0.7 percent), and the average for all developing countries (0.3 percent).

Larger countries naturally tend to have lower trade ratios than smaller countries because they have more natural resources and greater opportunities for economies of scale and internal trade.[1] Following Pritchett (1991), table I.18 shows estimates of trade openness ratios adjusted for structural factors (population, country size transportation costs (cif/fob factor), per capita income, and major resource endowments such as oil).[2] Regression results are described below. The residuals of the regression indicate by how much a country exceeds or falls short of the level of openness expected for a country of its type. In the 1990-94, time period, India and Pakistan's trade ratios were roughly what they should be for countries with their particular endowment; Bangladesh was less open while Sri Lanka was more open. China is much more open than would be predicted, while the United States and Japan are less open.[3]

Comparisons among countries, using market exchange rates, may be misleading, because non-tradable goods tend to have lower relative prices in developing countries than in developed countries[4]. The answer is to use purchasing power parity-adjusted GDP. The last column in table I.18 reports the results of re-estimating the trade openness ratios adjusted for population and other factors, but using trade to GDP ratios, PPP adjusted, income data, as developed by Summers and Heston.[5] Differences with the previous estimates are minor. India looks now marginally less open than it should be and Pakistan marginally more open.

Regression results of adjusting trade to GDP ratios for structural characteristics. Are presented below Regression 1 is the basic equation that relates trade to GDP ratios to population, area, a proxy for transportation costs (given by the difference between the merchandise import and export prices), GDP per capita and GDP per capita squared (to test the hypothesis that the trade to GDP ratio increases at a decreasing rate in GDP per capita) and an oil dummy (oil exporters are those with greater than 30 percent of oil exports). Regression 2 contains the same variables as Regression 1 on the right hand side but has the trade to GDP ratio evaluated in PPP values on the left hand side. Both regression are estimated in log form.

---

[1] However, size, measured in terms of land or population, would affect the level of trade openness but not the rate of change as the relative size of a country and its factor endowments remain relatively constant over time.

[2] See Pritchett (1991), Balassa (1988), and Syrquin and Chenery (1989) for a comprehensive discussion of measures of openness.

[3] Estimates of openness should be taken with a pinch of salt because: the standard error of the regression is large, casting doubts on the reliability of the estimated adjusted values for each individual country; and because there is a small number of big countries, the standard error of the population variable is large. Thus, while the coefficient appears to be significantly different from zero, it is not estimated precisely. (Some of the weaknesses related to the methodology of estimating adjusted trade ratios are discussed in Pritchett, 1991). Furthermore, the standard prediction for an outlier (a very large or a very small country) is even greater.

[4] See Rogoff (1996) for an extensive discussion of issues associated with purchasing power parity.

[5] Summers and Heston (1988). Periodic updates of data provided electronically; the latest version is version 5.6.

Data sources. Trade to GDP ratios, real GDP per capita, population, area and oil dummy are from World Bank sources including the Bank Economic and Social Database, the DEC Analytical Database and the World Development Report. Transportation costs (cif/fob factor) is from the International Monetary Fund's International Financial Statistics. Trade to GDP ratios measured in purchasing power parities are from Summers and Heston, version 5.6.

Regression 1

Dependent variable:	X+M/GDP			
Number of observations:		114		

Mean of dependent variable:	4.0834	Adjusted R=squared:	0.45166
Std. dev. of dependent var:	0.5916	Durbin-Watson:	1.98674
Sum of squared residuals:	20.5339	F-statistic (zero slopes):	16.51270
Variance of residuals:	0.1919	Schwarz Bayes Info Crit.:	-1.42330
Std. error of regression:	0.4381	Log of likelihood function:	-64.05420
R-squared:	0.4808		

Estimated Variable	Standard Coefficient	Error	t-statistic
C	5.8129	0.4453	13.0552
Pop	-0.1479	0.0358	-4.1316
Area	-0.0994	0.0276	-3.6003
Cif-fob	-0.4134	0.7339	-0.5632
GDPpc	24.4717	52.3701	0.4673
GDPpc2	-12.2232	26.1831	-0.4668
Oildum	0.3440	0.1425	2.4135

Regression 2

Dependent variable:	X+M/GDP PPP			
Number of observations:		101		

Mean of dependent variable:	4.0524	Adjusted R=squared:	0.45442
Std. dev. of dependent var:	0.5393	Durbin-Watson:	1.70962
Sum of squared residuals:	14.9176	F-statistic (zero slopes):	14.88200
Variance of residuals:	0.1587	Schwarz Bayes Info Crit.:	-1.59272
Std. error of regression:	0.3984	Log of likelihood function:	-46.72750
R-squared:	0.4872		

Estimated Variable	Standard Coefficient	Error	t-statistic
C	5.4396	0.4126	13.1827
Pop	-0.0942	0.0347	-2.7164
Area	-0.1392	0.0283	-4.9242
Cif-fob	-0.5825	0.6992	-0.8331
GDPpc	-15.6316	63.1505	-0.2475
GDPpc2	7.8344	31.5735	0.2481
Oildum	0.3046	0.1727	1.7639

Developing Countries

Country	X+M/GDP Ranking	Residual	Predicted	Predicted %	X+M/GDP PPP Ranking	Residual	Predicted	Predicted %	X+M/GDP Ranking	Unadjusted %
Malaysia	1	1.14646	3.94651	51.75	1	1.12826	3.94441	51.65	6	162.87
Singapore	2	0.97226	4.85486	128.36	2	0.87093	5.00666	149.40	1	339.38
Hong Kong	3	0.88019	4.72734	112.99	4	0.69898	4.91484	136.30	2	272.47
Sudan	4	0.87594	3.6707	39.28	89	-0.43438	3.60575	36.81	20	94.31
Guyana	5	0.73496	4.40174	81.59	81	-0.27545	4.23664	69.18	5	170.15
Botswana	6	0.64069	4.22364	68.28		.	.	.	11	129.58
Thailand	7	0.63453	3.72464	41.46	6	0.59369	3.74712	42.40	30	78.19
Jordan	8	0.60757	4.30358	73.96	3	0.71214	4.25913	70.75	8	135.80
China	9	0.59507	2.98347	19.76	14	0.37056	2.9988	20.06	99	35.82
Egypt	10	0.56744	3.64375	38.23	7	0.58438	3.6369	37.97	43	67.44
Zaire	11	0.55121	3.55008	34.82		.	.		52	60.42
Mauritania	12	0.46565	4.12615	61.94	5	0.68118	3.90583	49.69	18	98.67

Country										
Lesotho	13	0.46418	4.46857	87.23	9	0.52854	4.46921	87.29	7	138.76
Philippines	14	0.42365	3.76972	43.37	18	0.33043	3.79622	44.53	46	66.25
Papua New Guinea	15	0.42068	4.09431	60.00	8	0.54332	3.99816	54.50	21	91.38
Kenya	17	0.40043	3.7476	42.42	24	0.27771	3.75369	42.68	50	63.31
Tunisia	19	0.37106	4.12176	61.67	19	0.31501	4.11461	61.23	23	89.37
Tanzania	21	0.35033	3.73433	41.86					56	59.42
Congo	22	0.33042	4.17923	65.32	15	0.35888	4.03668	56.64	22	90.89
Zimbabwe	23	0.31841	3.97438	53.22	21	0.30783	3.89537	49.17	35	73.17
Nigeria	24	0.31494	3.87979	48.41	17	0.34149	3.87713	48.29	45	66.34
Taiwan	25	0.28611	4.18301	65.56	31	0.20704	4.29143	73.07	24	87.28
Zambia	26	0.27779	3.93796	51.31	13	0.39778	3.77291	43.51	42	67.74
Saudi Arabia'	27	0.27169	4.1379	62.67					26	82.24
Malawi	28	0.26049	3.84045	46.55	29	0.22954	3.85862	47.40	53	60.40
Jamaica	29	0.24562	4.55439	95.05	30	0.22073	4.57267	96.80	13	121.51
The Gambia	30	0.23046	4.63548	103.08	20	0.30848	4.59917	99.40	10	129.79
Paraguay	31	0.22334	4.09345	59.95	34	0.14887	4.00343	54.79	33	74.95
Mali	32	0.21531	3.72485	41.47	22	0.30657	3.61639	37.20	71	51.43
Sri Lanka	33	0.20751	4.07533	58.87	36	0.1307	4.10239	60.48	37	72.45
Indonesia	34	0.19871	3.71687	41.14	27	0.2598	3.73638	41.95	75	50.18
Chile	35	0.17273	3.90905	49.85	23	0.27896	3.85556	47.26	57	59.25
Cote d'Ivoire	36	0.17215	3.92351	50.58	26	0.26661	3.87398	48.13	54	60.08
Angola	37	0.17195	4.1577	63.92					32	75.92
Chad	39	0.13961	3.89757	49.28	11	0.484	3.60315	36.71	63	56.67
Korea	40	0.096744	3.96687	52.82	44	0.045714	4.07884	59.08	59	58.18
Morocco	41	0.089573	3.84301	46.67	37	0.13002	3.82122	45.66	72	51.04
Fiji	42	0.088488	4.67785	107.54	33	0.16737	4.6177	101.26	15	117.49
Pakistan	43	0.08633	3.50768	33.37	46	0.019147	3.60172	36.66	98	36.38
Honduras	44	0.086044	4.20856	67.26	41	0.094094	4.15054	63.47	34	73.30
South Africa	45	0.081768	3.69905	40.41	38	0.12433	3.68721	39.93	86	43.85
Czech Republic	46	0.076431	4.18819	65.90					38	71.14
Somalia	49	0.05026	3.95009	51.94					66	54.62
Ecuador	50	0.047627	4.00433	54.84	35	0.14628	3.95173	52.03	61	57.51
United Arab Emirates	51	0.035945	4.76939	117.85					12	122.16
Poland	52	0.030164	3.82815	45.98	66	-0.12679	3.86826	47.86	80	47.39
Malta	53	0.023274	5.23046	186.88					4	191.28
Mauritius	54	0.017924	4.86333	129.45	51	0.002834	4.90488	134.95	9	131.80
Costa Rica	55	0.015488	4.3844	80.19	50	0.009429	4.35774	78.08	27	81.44
Nicaragua	56	0.008022	4.23434	69.02	43	0.048619	4.17953	65.34	39	69.57
Liberia	58	-0.00469	4.29081	73.03					36	72.68
Senegal	59	-0.00992	4.08156	59.24	56	-0.049993	4.02443	55.95	58	58.65
India	61	-0.01639	3.06317	21.40	73	-0.21244	3.20165	24.57	110	21.05
Panama	62	-0.01695	4.37668	79.57	53	-0.00819	4.31859	75.08	29	78.24
Hungary	65	-0.03315	4.17749	65.20	55	-0.010837	4.21836	67.92	51	63.08
Iran	67	-0.07199	3.94262	51.55	88	-0.40046	3.89363	49.09	79	47.97
Bahrain	68	-0.09925	5.46361	235.95					3	213.66
Benin	69	-0.10111	4.1406	62.84	63	-0.11212	4.10757	60.80	62	56.80
Togo	71	-0.10493	4.30188	73.84	28	0.23907	4.22131	68.12	44	66.48
Madagascar	72	-0.11358	3.89377	49.10	48	0.018134	3.73536	41.90	88	43.82
Ghana	73	-0.11592	3.9918	54.15	75	-0.24015	3.94318	51.58	78	48.23
Greece	74	-0.13049	4.12799	62.05	68	-0.13041	4.1361	62.56	67	54.46
Algeria	75	-0.13672	4.04689	57.22	47	0.018376	3.94148	51.49	76	49.91
Mexico	76	-0.14769	3.56282	35.26	62	-0.10974	3.56889	35.48	104	30.42
Bolivia	77	-0.15154	3.93134	50.98	61	-0.070922	3.83259	46.18	89	43.81
Venezuela	78	-0.15157	4.17233	64.87	57	-0.059419	4.10124	60.42	65	55.74
Cameroon	81	-0.16912	3.94954	51.91	72	-0.16138	3.88996	48.91	87	43.83
Nepal	82	-0.16914	3.90885	49.84					91	42.09
Colombia	83	-0.17374	3.72156	41.33	69	-0.14194	3.70128	40.50	100	34.74
Romania	84	-0.18896	4.09626	60.12					77	49.76
Turkey	85	-0.20068	3.69873	40.40	45	0.029018	3.72915	41.64	101	33.05
Israel	90	-0.23918	4.45971	86.46	85	-0.32822	4.5156	91.43	41	68.07
Gabon	91	-0.24487	4.69132	109.00	71	-0.15979	4.49498	89.57	25	85.32
Dominican Republic	92	-0.25911	4.23892	69.33	65	-0.1215	4.22183	68.16	69	53.51
Burkina Faso	93	-0.28252	3.93435	51.13	64	-0.11262	3.86963	47.92	96	38.55
Kuwait	94	-0.28884	4.95896	142.45					16	106.71

Annex I.II Adjusted trade to GDP ratios: regression results

Guatemala	95	-0.31604	4.1147	61.23	86	-0.36839	4.1193	61.52	84	44.64
Niger	96	-0.35292	3.81071	45.18	.	.	.		102	31.75
Bangladesh	97	-0.35881	3.69196	40.12	92	-0.52706	3.7951	44.48	106	28.03
Central African Republic	98	-0.36339	4.09738	60.18	77	-0.2468	3.96062	52.49	93	41.85
Sierra Leone	99	-0.37594	4.2216	68.14	83	-0.28885	4.17637	65.13	81	46.79
Rwanda	100	-0.37706	4.17578	65.09	98	-0.85381	4.14854	63.34	83	44.64
El Salvador	101	-0.43379	4.36425	78.59	97	-0.65529	4.40738	82.05	73	50.93
Ethiopia	102	-0.46172	3.62899	37.67	.	.	.		108	23.74
Uruguay	103	-0.53075	4.28428	72.55	90	-0.44188	4.22948	68.68	90	42.67
Peru	104	-0.54823	3.73035	41.69	91	-0.48743	3.64485	38.28	107	24.10
Uganda	105	-0.55221	3.92519	50.66	96	-0.64635	3.94884	51.88	105	29.17
Brazil	106	-0.55872	3.30491	27.25	94	-0.59457	3.28582	26.73	112	15.58
Suriname	108	-0.60427	4.56114	95.69	.	.	.		70	52.29
Burundi	109	-0.62949	4.31088	74.51	95	-0.63801	4.26767	71.36	94	39.70
Barbados	110	-0.66515	5.23915	188.51	.	.	.		19	96.93
Haiti	112	-0.8055	4.23231	68.88	.	.	.		103	30.78
Argentina	113	-0.9618	3.65389	38.62	100	-0.88406	3.60404	36.75	113	14.76
Myanmar(Burma)	114	-2.05674	3.68421	39.81	.	.	.		114	5.09

Industrial Countries

Canada	16	0.40674	3.62485	37.52	12	0.40671	3.54241	34.55	64	56.35
Ireland	18	0.37186	4.39899	81.37	16	0.35006	4.39904	81.37	14	118.02
Netherlands	20	0.35364	4.25383	70.37	25	0.26905	4.3611	78.34	17	100.23
Norway	38	0.14543	4.23971	69.39	32	0.18759	4.19831	66.57	28	80.25
Austria	47	0.068693	4.27589	71.94	42	0.050953	4.31558	74.86	31	77.06
United Kingdom	48	0.05734	3.87036	47.96	60	-0.069663	3.97325	53.16	74	50.79
France	57	0.001848	3.79499	44.48	58	-0.06148	3.86925	47.91	85	44.56
Sweden	60	-0.0149	4.10591	60.70	59	-0.065223	4.0895	59.71	55	59.80
Portugal	63	-0.01747	4.17978	65.35	39	0.11823	4.20192	66.81	49	64.22
Germany	64	-0.03059	3.86551	47.73	40	0.11144	3.97923	53.48	82	46.29
Australia	66	-0.07039	3.69286	40.16	54	-0.00831	3.5871	36.13	97	37.43
Italy	70	-0.10129	3.83848	46.45	76	-0.24235	3.93073	50.94	92	41.98
Switzerland	79	-0.15875	4.39372	80.94	74	-0.21616	4.46608	87.01	40	69.06
Spain	80	-0.16219	3.8352	46.30	78	-0.25199	3.88112	48.48	95	39.37
New Zealand	86	-0.20589	4.25872	70.72	70	-0.14342	4.19556	66.39	60	57.56
Finland	87	-0.21112	4.20343	66.92	82	-0.2834	4.16517	64.40	68	54.18
U.S.A	88	-0.22082	3.29813	27.06	80	-0.26528	3.34029	28.23	109	21.70
Denmark	89	-0.23201	4.40532	81.89	79	-0.2542	4.4511	85.72	47	64.93
Iceland	107	-0.57651	4.74364	114.85	87	-0.38347	4.58681	98.18	48	64.53
Japan	111	-0.80268	3.70739	40.75	99	-0.87411	3.83266	46.19	111	18.26

ANNEX II.I

PRIVATE CAPITAL FLOWS

Table II.1 Aggregate net long-term resource flows to developing countries, 1990-1996

(US$ billions)	Average 1980-89	1990	1991	1992	1993	1994	1995	1996[a]
All Developing Countries								
Aggregate net resource flows	78.2	100.6	122.5	146.0	212.0	207.0	237.2	284.6
Official development finance	37.8	56.3	65.6	55.4	55.0	45.7	53.0	40.8
Official grants	14.3	29.2	37.3	31.6	29.3	32.4	32.6	31.3
Official loans	23.5	27.1	28.3	23.8	25.7	13.2	20.4	9.5
Bilateral	11.9	11.6	13.3	11.3	10.3	2.9	9.4	-5.6
Multilateral	11.6	15.5	15.0	12.5	15.4	10.3	11.0	15.0
Total private flows	40.4	44.4	56.9	90.6	157.1	161.3	184.2	243.8
Private debt flows	27.4	16.6	16.2	35.9	44.9	44.9	56.6	88.6
Commercial banks	17.7	3.0	2.8	12.5	-0.3	11.0	26.4	34.2
Bonds	2.0	2.3	10.1	9.9	35.9	29.3	28.5	46.1
Others	7.8	11.3	3.3	13.5	9.2	4.6	1.7	8.3
Foreign direct investment	12.3	24.5	33.5	43.6	67.2	83.7	95.5	109.5
Portfolio equity investment	0.6	3.2	7.2	11.0	45.0	32.7	32.1	45.7

a. Preliminary

Source: World Bank Debtor Reporting System

Table II.2 Aggregate net long-term resource flows to South Asia, 1980 - 1996

(US$ billions)	Average 1980-89	1990	1991	1992	1993	1994	1995	1996[a]
South Asia								
Aggregate net resource flows	8.6	9.2	10.7	10.0	11.8	14.4	8.4	17.0
Official development finance	5.9	7.1	8.8	7.1	5.8	6.0	3.2	6.4
Official grants	2.4	2.4	3.4	2.5	2.2	2.6	2.5	2.5
Official loans	3.4	4.6	5.3	4.6	3.6	3.4	0.7	3.9
Bilateral	1.1	1.2	-0.9	1.2	0.7	0.4	-1.0	1.1
Multilateral	2.3	3.4	4.0	3.4	2.8	3.0	1.7	2.8
Total private flows	2.7	2.2	1.9	2.9	6.0	8.5	5.2	10.7
Private debt flows	2.4	1.6	1.5	1.9	3.1	1.0	1.1	2.6
Commercial banks	1.7	1.6	0.3	2.2	1.3	-0.1	0.5	3.0
Bonds	0.2	0.1	1.4	-0.2	0.5	0.2	0.2	-0.8
Others	0.4	-0.1	-0.2	0.0	1.4	0.9	0.4	0.5
Foreign direct investment	0.0	0.5	0.5	0.6	0.8	1.2	1.8	2.6
Portfolio equity investment	0.0	0.1	0.0	0.4	2.0	6.2	2.3	5.4

a. Preliminary

Source: World Bank Debtor Reporting System

Table II.3 Net resource flows to developing countries, by region and type, 1990 - 1996

(US$ billions)	1990	1991	1992	1993	1994	1995	1996 [a]
All developing countries	100.6	122.5	146.0	212.0	207.0	237.2	284.6
Official	56.3	65.6	55.4	55.0	45.7	53.0	40.8
Private	44.4	56.9	90.6	157.1	161.3	184.2	243.8
FDI	24.5	33.5	43.6	67.2	83.7	95.5	109.5
Portfolio equity	3.2	7.2	11.0	45.0	32.7	32.1	45.7
Other private	16.6	16.2	35.9	44.9	44.9	56.6	88.6
Sub-Saharan Africa	17.2	16.2	15.8	14.1	20.7	23.2	26.1
Official	17.0	15.3	16.1	14.6	15.5	14.0	14.3
Private	0.2	0.8	-0.3	-0.5	5.2	9.1	11.8
FDI	0.9	1.6	0.8	1.6	3.1	2.2	2.6
Portfolio equity	0.0	0.0	0.1	0.2	0.9	4.9	3.6
Other private	-0.7	-0.8	-1.3	-2.3	1.2	2.1	5.6
East Asia & Pacific	27.3	29.5	45.5	73.0	79.6	95.8	116.1
Official	7.9	8.7	8.6	10.6	8.5	11.6	7.3
Private	19.3	20.8	36.9	62.4	71.0	84.1	108.7
FDI	10.2	12.7	20.9	38.1	44.1	51.8	61.2
Portfolio equity	1.7	0.7	2.1	14.6	10.1	14.7	12.9
Other private	7.4	7.4	13.9	9.7	16.8	17.6	34.6
Europe & Central Asia	15.1	24.0	34.4	38.6	28.8	40.6	45.3
Official	5.6	16.1	12.7	13.0	11.6	10.5	14.1
Private	9.5	7.9	21.8	25.6	17.2	30.1	31.2
FDI	2.1	4.4	6.3	8.4	8.1	17.2	15.0
Portfolio equity	0.2	0.0	0.1	1.0	2.3	2.8	6.7
Other private	7.2	3.5	15.4	16.2	6.9	10.1	9.5
Latin America & the Caribbean	21.6	30.6	32.5	65.1	54.9	66.9	69.2
Official	9.1	7.6	3.9	5.3	1.3	12.6	-5.3
Private	12.5	22.9	28.7	59.8	53.6	54.3	74.4
FDI	8.1	12.5	12.7	14.1	24.2	22.9	25.9
Portfolio equity	1.1	6.2	8.2	27.2	13.2	7.2	16.5
Other private	3.3	4.2	7.7	18.5	16.2	24.2	32.0
Middle East & North Africa	10.2	11.3	7.6	9.5	8.6	2.4	10.9
Official	9.6	9.1	7.1	5.6	2.7	1.0	4.0
Private	0.6	2.2	0.5	3.9	5.8	1.4	6.9
FDI	2.8	1.8	2.2	4.2	3.0	-0.3	2.2
Portfolio equity	0.0	0.0	0.0	0.0	0.1	0.2	0.7
Other private	-2.1	0.4	-1.7	-0:3	2.8	1.6	4.0
South Asia	9.2	10.7	10.0	11.8	14.4	8.4	17.0
Official	7.1	8.8	7.1	5.8	6.0	3.2	6.4
Private	2.2	1.9	2.9	6.0	8.5	5.2	10.7
FDI	0.5	0.5	0.6	0.8	1.2	1.8	2.6

Portfolio equity	0.1	0.0	0.4	2.0	6.2	2.3	5.4
Other private	1.6	1.5	1.9	3.1	1.0	1.1	2.6
Afghanistan (US$ million)	104.7	641.3	179.1	153.5	363.7	169.2	249.0
Official	104.7	641.3	179.1	125.5	363.7	169.2	249.0
Private	0.0	0.0	0.0	28.0	0.0	0.0	0.0
FDI	0.0	0.0	0.0	0.0	0.0	0.0	0.0
Portfolio equity	0.0	0.0	0.0	0.0	0.0	0.0	0.0
Other private	0.0	0.0	0.0	28.0	0.0	0.0	0.0
Bangladesh (US$ millions)	1,708.4	1,684.4	1,440.1	1,029.9	1,485.2	906.0	1,247.0
Official	1,638.4	1,648.2	1,423.4	1,023.3	1,455.2	895.8	1,203.0
Private	70.0	36.2	16.7	6.6	30.0	10.2	44.0
FDI	3.0	1.0	4.0	14.0	11.0	2.0	15.0
Portfolio equity	0.0	0.0	0.0	0.0	0.0	0.0	0.0
Other private	67.0	35.2	12.7	-7.4	19.0	8.2	29.0
Bhutan (US$ millions)	0.02	0.04	0.03	0.03	0.04	0.04	0.04
Official	0.03	0.04	0.04	0.04	0.05	0.04	0.04
Private	0.00	0.00	0.00	0.00	0.00	0.00	0.00
FDI	0.00	0.00	0.00	0.00	0.00	0.00	0.00
Portfolio equity	0.00	0.00	0.00	0.00	0.00	0.00	0.00
Other private	0.00	0.00	0.00	0.00	0.00	0.00	0.00
India (US$ millions)	4.7	5.0	4.9	6.8	7.9	3.3	9.7
Official	2.9	3.5	3.1	2.3	1.5	-0.3	1.7
Private	1.9	1.6	1.7	4.6	6.4	3.6	8.0
FDI	0.2	0.1	0.2	0.3	0.6	1.3	2.3
Portfolio equity	0.1	0.0	0.2	1.8	4.7	1.5	4.6
Other private	1.6	1.4	1.3	2.5	1.1	0.8	1.1
Maldives (US$ millions)	0.02	0.03	0.03	0.04	0.03	0.06	0.04
Official	0.02	0.02	0.02	0.03	0.02	0.05	0.03
Private	0.01	0.01	0.01	0.01	0.01	0.01	0.01
FDI	0.01	0.01	0.01	0.01	0.01	0.01	0.01
Portfolio equity	0.00	0.00	0.00	0.00	0.00	0.00	0.00
Other private	0.00	0.00	0.00	0.00	0.00	0.00	0.00
Nepal (US$ millions)	0.3	0.3	0.3	0.3	0.3	0.3	0.3
Official	0.3	0.3	0.3	0.3	0.3	0.3	0.3
Private	0.0	0.0	0.0	0.0	0.0	0.0	0.0
FDI	0.0	0.0	0.0	0.0	0.0	0.0	0.0
Portfolio equity	0.0	0.0	0.0	0.0	0.0	0.0	0.0
Other private	0.0	0.0	0.0	0.0	0.0	0.0	0.0
Pakistan (US$ millions)	1.4	1.7	2.4	2.4	3.1	2.5	4.0
Official	1.2	1.5	1.3	1.2	1.4	1.1	1.6
Private	0.2	0.2	1.1	1.2	1.8	1.4	2.4
FDI	0.2	0.3	0.3	0.3	0.4	0.4	0.2
Portfolio equity	0.0	0.0	0.1	0.2	1.3	0.7	0.7
Other private	-0.1	-0.1	0.6	0.7	0.0	0.3	1.5

Sri Lanka (US$ millions)	0.6	0.8	0.4	0.6	0.7	0.6	0.9
Official	0.5	0.7	0.3	0.5	0.4	0.5	0.7
Private	0.1	0.1	0.1	0.1	0.2	0.1	0.3
FDI	0.0	0.0	0.1	0.2	0.2	0.1	0.1
Portfolio equity	0.0	0.0	0.0	0.0	0.1	0.6	0.1
Other private	0.0	0.0	0.0	-0.1	0.0	-0.5	0.1

a. Preliminary
Source: World Bank Debtor Reporting System

Table II.4 Composition of total external capital flows to developing countries, 1990 - 1996

(percent)	1990	1991	1992	1993	1994	1995	1996 [a]
All developing countries (US$ bn)	100.6	122.5	146.0	212.0	207.0	237.2	284.6
Official	55.9	53.6	38.0	25.9	22.1	22.3	14.3
Private	44.1	46.4	62.0	74.1	77.9	77.7	85.7
FDI	24.4	27.3	29.9	31.7	40.4	40.3	38.5
Portfolio equity	3.2	5.9	7.5	21.2	15.8	13.5	16.1
Other private	16.5	13.2	24.6	21.2	21.7	23.9	31.1
Sub-Saharan Africa (US$ mn)	17.1	13.2	10.8	6.6	10.0	9.8	9.2
Official	16.9	12.5	11.0	6.9	7.5	5.9	5.0
Private	0.2	0.7	-0.2	-0.2	2.5	3.8	4.1
FDI	0.9	1.3	0.6	0.8	1.5	0.9	0.9
Portfolio equity	0.0	0.0	0.1	0.1	0.4	2.1	1.2
Other private	-0.7	-0.6	-0.9	-1.1	0.6	0.9	2.0
East Asia & Pacific (US$ mn)	27.1	24.1	31.2	34.4	38.4	40.4	40.8
Official	7.9	7.1	5.9	5.0	4.1	4.9	2.6
Private	19.2	17.0	25.3	29.4	34.3	35.5	38.2
FDI	10.1	10.4	14.3	18.0	21.3	21.8	21.5
Portfolio equity	1.7	0.6	1.4	6.9	4.9	6.2	4.5
Other private	7.3	6.0	9.5	4.6	8.1	7.4	12.2
Europe & Central Asia (US$ mn)	15.0	19.6	23.6	18.2	13.9	17.1	15.9
Official	5.5	13.2	8.7	6.2	5.6	4.4	5.0
Private	9.5	6.4	14.9	12.1	8.3	12.7	11.0
FDI	2.1	3.6	4.3	4.0	3.9	7.3	5.3
Portfolio equity	0.2	0.0	0.0	0.5	1.1	1.2	2.4
Other private	7.1	2.9	10.5	7.6	3.3	4.2	3.3
Latin America & the Caribbean (US$ mn)	21.5	24.9	22.3	30.7	26.5	28.2	24.3
Official	9.1	6.2	2.6	2.5	0.6	5.3	-1.9
Private	12.4	18.7	19.6	28.2	25.9	22.9	26.2
FDI	8.1	10.2	8.7	6.6	11.7	9.7	9.1
Portfolio equity	1.1	5.1	5.6	12.8	6.4	3.0	5.8

Other private	3.2	3.4	5.3	8.7	7.8	10.2	11.3
Middle East & North Africa (US$ mn)	10.1	9.2	5.2	4.5	4.1	1.0	3.8
Official		7.4	4.9	2.6	1.3	0.4	1.4
Private		1.8	0.3	1.8	2.8	0.6	2.4
FDI		1.5	1.5	2.0	1.4	-0.1	0.8
Portfolio equity		0.0	0.0	0.0	0.1	0.1	0.2
Other private		0.3	-1.2	-0.1	1.3	0.7	1.4
South Asia (US$ mn)		8.7	6.8	5.5	7.0	3.5	6.0
Official		7.2	4.9	2.7	2.9	1.4	2.2
Private		1.6	2.0	2.8	4.1	2.2	3.8
FDI		0.4	0.4	0.4	0.6	0.8	0.9
Portfolio equity		0.0	0.3	1.0	3.0	1.0	1.9
Other private		1.2	1.3	1.5	0.5	0.4	0.9
Afghanistan (US$ mn)		523.5	122.7	72.4	175.7	71.3	87.5
Official		523.5	122.7	59.2	175.7	71.3	87.5
Private		0.0	0.0	13.2	0.0	0.0	0.0
FDI		0.0	0.0	0.0	0.0	0.0	0.0
Portfolio equity		0.0	0.0	0.0	0.0	0.0	0.0
Other private		0.0	0.0	13.2	0.0	0.0	0.0
Bangladesh (US$ mn)		1374.9	986.6	485.7	717.6	382.0	438.2
Official		1345.3	975.1	482.6	703.1	377.7	422.7
Private		29.5	11.4	3.1	14.5	4.3	15.5
FDI		0.8	2.7	6.6	5.3	0.8	5.3
Portfolio equity		0.0	0.0	0.0	0.0	0.0	0.0
Other private		28.7	8.7	-3.5	9.2	3.4	10.2
Bhutan (US$ mn)		0.0	0.0	0.0	0.0	0.0	0.0
Official		0.0	0.0	0.0	0.0	0.0	0.0
Private		0.0	0.0	0.0	0.0	0.0	0.0
FDI		0.0	0.0	0.0	0.0	0.0	0.0
Portfolio equity		0.0	0.0	0.0	0.0	0.0	0.0
Other private		0.0	0.0	0.0	0.0	0.0	0.0
India (US$ mn)		4.1	3.3	3.2	3.8	1.4	3.4
Official		2.8	2.2	1.1	0.7	-0.1	0.6
Private		1.3	1.2	2.2	3.1	1.5	2.8
FDI		0.1	0.1	0.1	0.3	0.5	0.8
Portfolio equity		0.0	0.2	0.9	2.3	0.6	1.6
Other private		1.2	0.9	1.2	0.5	0.3	0.4
Maldives (US$ mn)		0.0	0.0	0.0	0.0	0.0	0.0
Official		0.0	0.0	0.0	0.0	0.0	0.0
Private		0.0	0.0	0.0	0.0	0.0	0.0
FDI		0.0	0.0	0.0	0.0	0.0	0.0

Portfolio equity	0.0	0.0	0.0	0.0	0.0	0.0
Other private	0.0	0.0	0.0	0.0	0.0	0.0
Nepal (US$ mn)	0.2	0.2	0.1	0.1	0.1	0.1
Official	0.2	0.2	0.1	0.2	0.1	0.1
Private	0.0	0.0	0.0	0.0	0.0	0.0
FDI	0.0	0.0	0.0	0.0	0.0	0.0
Portfolio equity	0.0	0.0	0.0	0.0	0.0	0.0
Other private	0.0	0.0	0.0	0.0	0.0	0.0
Pakistan (US$ mn)	1.4	1.7	1.1	1.5	1.1	1.4
Official	1.2	0.9	0.6	0.7	0.5	0.6
Private	0.2	0.7	0.6	0.9	0.6	0.8
FDI	0.2	0.2	0.2	0.2	0.2	0.1
Portfolio equity	0.0	0.1	0.1	0.6	0.3	0.2
Other private	0.0	0.4	0.3	0.0	0.1	0.5
Sri Lanka (US$ mn)	0.7	0.3	0.3	0.3	0.3	0.3
Official	0.6	0.2	0.2	0.2	0.2	0.2
Private	0.1	0.1	0.1	0.1	0.1	0.1
FDI	0.0	0.1	0.1	0.1	0.0	0.0
Portfolio equity	0.0	0.0	0.0	0.1	0.3	0.0
Other private	0.0	0.0	0.0	0.0	-0.2	0.0

a. Preliminary

Source: World Bank Debtor Reporting System

Table II.5 Portfolio equity flows to developing countries, 1990 - 1996

(US$ millions)	1990	1991	1992	1993	1994	1995	1996 [a]
All developing countries	3,225	7,207	11,012	44,987	32,688	32,088	45,700
International issues	98	4,697	5,668	10,980	18,482	8,730	..
Local equity investment	3,127	2,510	5,344	34,007	14,206	23,357	..
Sub-Saharan Africa	0	0	144	174	860	4,869	3,500
International issues	0	0	144	126	638	393	..
Local equity investment	0	0	0	47	222	4,475	..
East Asia and Pacific	1,750	704	2,057	14,619	10,088	14,715	12,900
International issues	0	0	1,302	2,635	6,818	6,317	..
Local equity investment	1,750	704	755	11,984	3,269	8,398	..
Europe and Central Asia	235	0	65	984	2,253	2,772	6,700
International issues	0	0	12	191	717	860	..
Local equity investment	235	0	53	793	1,535	1,912	..
Latin America and Caribbean	1,099	6,228	8,229	27,185	13,159	7,190	16,500

International issues	98	4,697	3,965	7,688	6,037	845	..
Local equity investment	1,001	1,531	4,265	19,498	7,123	6,345	..
Middle East & North Africa	0	0	0	0	106	203	700
International issues	0	0	0	0	0	34	..
Local equity investment	0	0	0	0	106	169	..
South Asia	105	23	380	2,025	6,223	2,341	5,400
International issues	0	0	246	340	4,271	281	..
Local equity investment	105	23	135	1,685	1,952	2,059	..
Bangladesh	0	0	0	0	48	33	30
International issues	0	0	0	0	26	7	..
Local equity investment	0	0	0	0	22	26	..
Bhutan	0	0	0	0	0	0	0
International issues	0	0	0	0	0	0	..
Local equity investment	0	0	0	0	0	0	..
India	105	0	241	1,840	4,729	1,517	5,600
International issues	0	0	240	340	3,029	274	..
Local equity investment	105	0	1	1,500	1,700	1,243	..
Maldives	0	0	0	0	0	0	0
International issues	0	0	0	0	0	0	..
Local equity investment	0	0	0	0	0	0	..
Nepal	0	0	0	0	0	0	0
International issues	0	0	0	0	0	0	..
Local equity investment	0	0	0	0	0	0	..
Pakistan	0	23	139	185	1,335	729	700
International issues	0	0	5	0	1,183	0	..
Local equity investment	0	23	134	185	151	729	..
Sri Lanka	0	0	0	0	112	61	70
International issues	0	0	0	0	33	0	..
Local equity investment	0	0	0	0	79	61	..
Afghanistan	0	0	0	0	0	0	0
International issues	0	0	0	0	0	0	..
Local equity investment	0	0	0	0	0	0	..

a. Preliminary
Source: World Bank Debtor Reporting System

Table II.6 Net foreign investment as a ratio of GNP, 1990-1996

(percentage)

	1990	1991	1992	1993	1994	1995	1996 [a]
All developing countries	0.6	0.8	1.0	1.5	1.8	1.8	1.9
Sub-Saharan Africa	0.3	0.6	0.3	0.6	1.2	0.8	0.8
East Asia and Pacific	1.6	1.8	2.7	4.5	4.4	4.2	4.2
South Asia	0.1	0.1	0.2	0.2	0.3	0.3	0.5
Europe & Central Asia	0.1	0.3	0.5	0.8	0.8	1.6	1.2
Latin America	0.8	1.2	1.1	1.1	1.6	1.5	1.6
North Africa & Middle East	0.6	0.4	0.5	0.9	0.6	-0.1	0.3
By income group:							
Low Income Countries	0.5	0.7	1.4	3.2	3.4	3.0	3.0
Middle Income Countries	0.6	0.8	0.9	1.0	1.2	1.4	1.4
Memo							
Low-income countries excluding China	0.2	0.5	0.5	0.8	0.9	0.8	0.9

a. Preliminary
Source: World Bank, Debtor Reporting System

Table II.7 International equity issues by developing countries and South Asia, 1990–1996

(US$ millions)

	1990	1991	1992	1993	1994	1995	1996 [a]
All developing countries	98	4,697	5,668	10,980	18,482	8,730	11,754
South Asia	0	0	246	340	4,271	281	1,340
Afghanistan	0	0	0	0	0	0	0
Bangladesh	0	0	0	0	26	7	0
Bhutan	0	0	0	0	0	0	0
India	0	0	240	340	3,029	274	1,340
Maldives	0	0	0	0	0	0	0
Nepal	0	0	0	0	0	0	0
Pakistan	0	0	5	0	1,183	0	0
Sri Lanka	0	0	0	0	33	0	0

a. Preliminary
Source: World Bank, Debtor Reporting System.

Table II.8 International bond issues by developing countries and South Asia, 1990–1996
(US$ millions)

	1990	1991	1992	1993	1994	1995	1996 [a]
All developing countries	4,683	8,303	21,114	47,104	40,874	45,456	81,669
South Asia	274	200	0	556	1,079	782	1,357
Afghanistan	0	0	0	0	0	0	0
Bangladesh	0	0	0	0	0	0	0
Bhutan	0	0	0	0	0	0	0
India	274	200	0	556	884	770	1,107
Maldives	0	0	0	0	0	0	0
Nepal	0	0	0	0	0	0	0
Pakistan	0	0	0	0	195	0	250
Sri Lanka	0	0	0	0	0	12	0

a. Preliminary.
Source: World Bank, Debtor Reporting System

Table II.9 Stock Market Capitalization: South Asian Countries
(US$ millions; end of period levels)

	1986	1987	1988	1989	1990	1991	1992	1993	1994	1995
Bangladesh	186	405	430	476	321	269	314	453	1,049	1,323
India	13,588	17,057	23,623	27,316	38,567	47,730	65,119	97,976	127,515	127,199
Nepal	-	-	-	-	-	-	-	-	264	244
Pakistan	1,710	1,960	2,460	2,457	2,850	7,326	8,029	11,602	12,263	9,286
Sri Lanka	421	608	471	427	917	1,936	1,439	2,498	2,884	1,998
All Emerging Markets	238,617	319,706	483,135	738,061	611,278	854,808	883,456	1,586,797	1,912,451	1,895,709
All Developed Markets	6,275,582	7,511,072	9,245,358	10,975,622	8,782,267	10,435,686	9,949,721	12,377,034	13,241,841	15,892,174
World Total	6,514,199	7,830,778	9,728,493	11,713,683	9,393,545	11,290,494	10,833,177	13,973,831	15,154,292	17,787,883

Note: Table contains year-end total market values of listed domestic companies.

Table II.10 Institutional Investor's Rating for South Asian Countries, 1980-96

	Mar 1980	Sept	Mar 1981	Sept	Mar 1982	Sept	Mar 1983	Sept	Mar 1984	Sept	Mar 1985	Sept	Mar 1986	Sept	Mar 1987	Sept	Mar 1988	Sept
Bangladesh	..	..	..	..	15.2	15.2	13.3	12.6	12.3	13.9	15.1	15.8	16.3	18.0	19.2	18.2	17.2	17.6
India	52.4	49.8	50	48.3	46.5	46.6	46.3	46.2	47.6	46.9	45.9	46.3	49.4	50.7	50 7	49.7	49.8	48.4
Nepal	..	..	..	..	.	.	..	..	..	..	.	.	..	.	..	.	22.8	24.1
Pakistan	21.4	20.3	22.1	21.3	21	22.2	21.5	20.4	21.1	23.8	26.2	27.7	28	29.8	30.4	30.0	31.2	31.1
Sri Lanka	..	..	..	..	30.4	30.4	30.2	29.7	27.5	26.3	25.8	23.9	24.9	24.6	25.1	23.5	23.1	22.7

	Mar 1989	Sept	Mar 1990	Sept	Mar 1991	Sept	Mar 1992	Sept	Mar 1993	Sept	Mar 1994	Sept	Mar 1995	Sept	Mar 1996	Sept
Bangladesh	17.7	18.4	18.3	17.8	18.4	16.4	17.2	17.1	19.3	18.7	20	23.2	24.8	25.6	26.5	26.9
India	47.8	47.9	47.9	46.2	44.3	38.4	37.6	37.5	38.6	38.4	40	42.2	44.2	46.1	45.8	46.3
Nepal	24.6	25.7	24.8	23.3	23.1	22.4	22.6	21.8	21.7	22.1	23.2	23.9	24.4	25.1	23.9	25.7
Pakistan	30.6	31.1	30.9	30.0	28.7	27.0	28	27.7	28.9	27.7	28.8	29.7	30.1	30.7	29.5	29.2
Sri Lanka	22.4	22.6	21.2	23.3	22	21.9	23.4	24.0	25.5	25.5	27.7	30.4	32.4	33.0	32.5	33.7

Source: *Institutional Investor, various issues.*

Table II.11 FDI to GDP ratios, 1975/79 to 1990/94

	Level 1975/79 %	Nominal level 1990/94 %	Annual average change (percentage points)
World	0.82	1.25	0.03
OECD	0.58	1.26	0.05
Other high income	1.85	3.60	0.12
Developing	0.84	1.18	0.02
East Asia	0.87	2.69	0.12
China	0.00	3.54	0.24
Indonesia	0.75	1.17	0.03
Malaysia	3.13	7.41	0.29
South Asia	0.10	0.44	0.02
India	0.00	0.14	0.01
Pakistan	0.13	0.51	0.03
Bangladesh	0.00	0.03	0.00
Sri Lanka	0.28	1.10	0.05
LAC	0.80	1.47	0.04
Brazil	1.06	0.38	-0.05
Mexico	0.73	1.46	0.05
Low-income countries	0.72	0.89	0.01
Large developing countries	0.38	1.33	0.06
Exporters of manufactures	0.69	1.70	0.07

Source: International Monetary Fund's International Financial Statistics,
World Bank data and staff estimates

Table II.12 Ratio of portfolio inflows to GDP, 1980/84 to 1990/94

	Nominal level 1980/84 %	Nominal level 1990-94 %	Average Annual Change (% points)
World	0.25	0.83	0.06
OECD	0.90	2.42	0.15
Developing	0.08	0.42	0.03
E Asia	0.54	0.52	0.00
China	0.01	0.37	0.04
Indonesia	0.17	0.32	0.02
Malaysia	2.44	-1.13	-0.36
S.Asia	0.00	0.33	0.03
India	0.00	0.62	0.06
Pakistan	0.01	0.94	0.09
Bangladesh	0.00	0.10	0.01
LAC	0.12	1.02	0.09
Brazil	-0.02	2.93	0.30
Mexico	0.04	4.24	0.42
MENA	0.09	0.04	0.00
ECA	0.06	1.08	0.10
SST	-0.01	0.05	0.01

Source: International Monetary Fund's International Financial Statistics,
World Bank Data and staff estimates.

Table II.13 India—Foreign direct investment: Actual flow during 1991-1995

Year	Actual* U.S.$ million	Approved* U.S.$ million	Actual as % approved investment
1991	154.5	324.8	47.6
1992	233.1	1,781.30	13.1
1993	573.8	3,558.50	16.1
1994	958.5	4,331.70	22.1
1995	1,986.40	11,245.00	17.7
Total	3,906.30	21,241.30	
Annual average	781.3	4,248.30	18.4

* Include data on NRI investments under the 40% and 100% schemes.

Annex II.14 India—Sectoral distribution of FDI

(percent)

Sectors		FDI outstanding by March 1990	FDI flows August 1991- June 1995
I.	Plantation	9.5	-
II.	Mining	0.3	-
III.	Petroleum	0.1	28.4
IV.	Manufacturing	84.9	58.8
	Food & beverages	7	8.2
	Textiles	4	3.9
	Transport equipment	12.3	5.3
	Machinery & mach. tool	15.4	4.5
	Metals & its products	6.1	7.9
	Electrical goods	12.8	2.9
	Chemicals and allied	33.4	9.8
	Others	8.8	6.3
V.	Services	5.2	13
	Total	100	100

Table II.15 India—Top ten industries with FDI approval between August 1991 and June 1995

Industry	% Share
1 Fuels (included Power)	28.39
2 Chemicals	8.36
3 Service sector	7.66
4 Metallurgical	7.36
5 Electrical equipment	6.50
6 Telecommunications	6.39
7 Food processing	5.96
8 Transportation	5.25
9 Hotel & Tourism	4.90
10 Textiles	3.91

Table II.16 India—Actual flows: share of different approval sources

(percent)

Sources of approval	1991	1992	1993	1994	1995
FIPB/SIA (Government)	54.37	70.23	54.55	49.85	60.74
RBI (automatic route)	0	6.99	13.35	12.06	8.32
NRI (Direct investment: 40% scheme + 100% scheme)	45.63	22.78	32.1	38.09	30.94
Total	100	100	100	100	100

Source: RBI, Annual reports

ANNEX II.II

EVOLUTION OF INVESTMENT AND REGULATORY REGIMES IN SOUTH ASIA

India. The investment and industrial regimes were significantly liberalized during the 1990s. Of particular importance was the decision to eliminate discriminatory treatment of enterprises with more than 40 percent of foreign equity and open a number of sectors to domestic and foreign private investors: power (March 1992); mining (March 1993); coal (March 1994); telecommunications (May 1994), and pharmaceuticals (September 1994). Prior government approval in decisions concerning expansion, diversification, merger, and acquisition was eliminated. Entry barriers were reduced to only a selected group of sectors, as shown in the following table. The convertibility of the rupee on current account was introduced in 1994. Fiscal incentives and concessions were replaced with straightforward cuts in tax rates: the corporate tax rate for foreign companies was reduced from 65 percent to 48 percent in 1997, whereas the comparable figure for domestic companies was lowered to 35 percent. Long-term capital gains tax also was reduced from 30 percent to 10 percent in 1997.

Substantial progress in FDI regime was also made in ***Pakistan.*** The investment regime was transformed from one emphasizing regulation and restriction to one featuring facilitation and promotion, including the establishment of the Pakistan Investment Board (PIB) in 1991. In addition, many regulatory deterrents to foreign investment were removed. These included: removal of government clearance requirement (except for certain sectors); relaxation of foreign ownership restrictions (with 100 percent foreign ownership allowed); relaxation of restrictions on foreign investor business (allowing trading activities); and, liberalization of foreign exchange/ regulations (e.g., open foreign currency accounts).

With the establishment of a Board of Investment (BOI) in 1989 and the liberalization of industrial policy since 1991, ***Bangladesh*** also significantly improved the regulatory environment, including allowing wholly foreign-owned joint ventures and abolishing performance requirements. New sectors have been progressively opened for foreign investment, with the telecommunication sector being opened for FDI in 1996. Most sectors (with the exception of arms, nuclear energy, forestry, railroad) are now available for direct foreign participation. ***Sri Lanka***, the country with the most open foreign investment regime (as perceived by multinational corporations), introduced a one-stop shop on foreign investment matters. In November 1995 the government strengthened preferential treatment for export-oriented, high-tech and high-value added sectors as well as large infrastructure projects.

Comparison of FDI Policies

	India	Pakistan	Sri Lanka	Bangladesh	Nepal
Barriers to entry	Closed defense products, atomic energy, coal and lignite, mineral oils, railway trans., radioactive materials Restricted:	Closed arms and ammunition security, printing, high explosives, radioactive materials	Restricted 15 sectors including fishing, professional services & mining	Closed: Defense equipment, international air transportation, railway transport, security, printing, forestry, nuclear energy.	Closed Small scale industries (exeption: foreign investors who do not require repatriation of income or invest- ment. In such cases up to 100% foreign equity is permitted).
Full foreign ownership requirements	35 priority, large scale export-oriented, and power enterprises may be 100% owned (with approval).	100% ownership allowed in all other sectors with approval	100% ownerships permitted with approval	100% ownership permitted with approval	100% equity permitted in large-scale industries. (SSI exception applies to MSI) subject to HSG's approval.
Performance Requirements	No local content requirements on new projects.	No requirements.	No requirements.	No requirements.	Nepalese workers must be employed after grace period (7 yrs.)
Transfer of Profits and Convertibility	Restrictions apply. Foreign exchange balancing mandate required for consumer goods sector	Restrictions apply. State bank approval needed in banking, insurance, airline and shipping sectors	No restrictions.	Restrictions apply. Provision for transfer subject to control by BOI and Central Bank	Restrictions apply. Repatriation instalments fixed by HMG.
Incentives	Export Processing Zones. Tax con- cessions for oil, power, shipping and air transport sectors	Export Processing Zone: Tax holidays, credits and rebates for exporters are available in certain sectors and designated regions	Export Processing Zones: Industrial parks. Tax concessions for exporters (>90%) large-scale advanced technology, small- scale infrastructure tourism, agriculture, and training facility sectors. Grants to electronics exporters. No tax holidays.	Export Processing Zones: Interest on foreign loans is tax exempt. Tax exemption on royalties, technical know-how, and technical assistance fees, and the facilities for their repatriation.	Export Processing Zone: 5-year tax holiday (additional up to 11 yrs) tax concessions to exporters (>90%).

ANNEX II.III

FOREIGN DIRECT INVESTMENTS IN SOUTH ASIAN COUNTRIES

INDIA

Overall trends. FDI inflows, as well as approved FDI, grew substantially since the early 1980s and the improvement in economic fundamentals and investment climate. The annual average amount of foreign equity investment approved during 1991-95, estimated at $3.5 billion, was about thirty-five times higher than the corresponding figure for the 1980s; and the actual flows of FDI reached nearly $2 billion in 1995. However, the actual flows as percentage of approved investment remains relatively low, at an average of 18 percent, which is about half the rate experienced in many developing countries (including China) actively seeking FDI inflows (table 2.4).

Table II.III-1 India—Foreign Direct Investment: Actual Flow During 1991-1995

Year	Actual* U.S.$ million	Actual change yearly %	Approved* U.S.$ million	Actual as % approved investment
1991	154.5		324.8	47.6
1992	233.1	50.9	1,781.3	13.1
1993	573.8	146.2	3,558.5	16.1
1994	958.5	67.0	4,331.7	22.1
1995	1,986.4	107.2	11,245.0	17.7
Total	3,906.3		21,241.3	
Annual average	781.3	92.8	4,248.3	18.4

* Include data on NRI investments under the 40% and 100% schemes.

Sectoral patterns. The distribution of FDI inflows by sector has changed considerably in recent years. The relative importance of the manufacturing sector, while continuing to be the single most significant FDI destination, has declined from 85% of FDI flows in 1990 to 59% by 1995 with the opening up of infrastructure and service sectors to direct foreign investment (table 2.5). Within the manufacturing itself, FDI flows appears to have shifted from heavy capital goods industries to light industries.

Table II.III-2 India—Sectoral distribution of FDI (percent)

Sectors	FDI outstanding by	FDI flows
I. Plantation	9.5	-
II. Mining	0.3	-
III. Petroleum	0.1	28.4
IV. Manufacturing	84.9	58.8
Food & beverages	7.0	8.2
Textiles	4.0	3.9
Transport equipment	12.3	5.3
Machinery & mach. tool	15.4	4.5
Metals & its products	6.1	7.9
Electrical goods	12.8	2.9
Chemicals and allied	33.4	9.8
Others	8.8	6.3
V. Services	5.2	13.0
Total	100.0	100.0

The top four industries—fuel (with a 28 percent share), chemical, services, and metals—account for more than 50 percent of the total FDI approved since 1991. The textile industry, an important source of exports, has attracted less than 4 percent of the total. It is noteworthy that FDI flows in India tend to focus on industries targeted at domestic markets, whereas China has been attracting FDI largely in export-oriented industries through special economic zones. Preliminary data for 1996 suggest that FDI in service sectors is growing fast. The share of FDI in telecommunications jumped to 24 percent of the total in 1996, thanks to the large foreign investment approved for the cellular mobile telephone sector.

Table II.III-3 India—Top ten industries receiving FDI approval between August 1991 and June 1995

Industry	Amount	% Share
1. Fuels (included Power)	99,601.85	28.39
2. Chemicals	29,314.09	8.36
3. Service sector	868.74	7.66
4. Metallurgical	25,802.64	7.36
5. Electrical equipment	22,799.82	6.50
6. Telecommunications	22,418.23	6.39
7. Food processing	20,912.99	5.96
8. Transportation	18,407.78	5.25
9. Hotel & Tourism	17,187.22	4.90
10. Textiles	13,710.87	3.91

Investment sources. The United States continues to be the leading source of FDI in India, accounting for 30.3 percent of the total FDI approved during the post-liberalization period (through 1995), up from 25.5 percent in the 1980s. FDI also originates from the United Kingdom (7.5 percent), Japan (5.0 percent), Switzerland (4.6 percent), and Germany (3.2 percent). In recent years the share of FDI from East Asia has increased considerably. According to the preliminary 1996 data, Korea became the second leading source of FDI in India in 1996 (with Rs. 22.8 billion approved), second only to the United States.

FDI flows to India can be classified as: (a) requiring prior Government clearance i.e. FIPB or SIA; (b) receiving automatic approval of the Reserve Bank of India (RBI); and (c) non-resident Indian (NRI) direct investment approval by RBI. It is interesting to note that the share of NRI has largely declined since 1991, possibly indicating that the liberalization policy has facilitated a further diversification of FDI sources (table 2.7). The distribution pattern shows the largest share of FDI under the category FIPB/SIA and an insignificant share under the RBI automatic approval route, which may reflect the large scale investment projects in a few sectors such as power and hydro-carbon.

Table II.III-4 India—Actual flows: share of different approval sources
(percent)

Sources of approval	1991	1992	1993	1994	1995
FIPB/SIA (Government)	54.37	70.23	54.55	49.85	60.74
RBI (automatic route)	0.00	6.99	13.35	12.06	8.32
NRI (Direct investment: 40% scheme + 100% scheme)	45.63	22.78	32.10	38.09	30.94
Total	100.00	100.00	100.00	100.00	100.00

PAKISTAN

Overall trends. Recent FDI inflows to Pakistan have followed a mild upward trend, with an average volume growing from about $100 million in much of the 1980s to an average of more than $300 million in the first half of 1990s, further to $750 million estimated for 1996. The growth of FDI inflows (as well as the size of flows) in Pakistan, however, has been less impressive than in India, possibly because of political uncertainties and relatively weak economic fundamentals.

Sectoral patterns. Foreign investors interest in sectors producing for export markets has been limited, with the exception of textiles and agribusiness. For example, approved projects in the Karachi Export Processing Zone (KEPZ) have totaled only less than $100 million since its inception in early 1980s. More recently, an increasing amount of foreign investment has been induced to service sectors, including privatization programs (e.g., banks) and infrastructure projects. Based on FDI stock figures (as of end-1993), manufacturing sectors account for about

60 percent of the total $650 million. The rest was largely accounted for by service sectors, with a negligible amount directed to agriculture and mining sectors.

Source countries. Roughly half of total FDI flows since the mid-1980s have come from the US, mostly in oil exploration projects. More recently, however, some diversification has occurred: in 1995 the US share of total FDI inflows in Pakistan has declined to less than one-third, while FDI from Japan, and Asian NIEs (notably, Hong Kong) have significantly increased. By contrast, the UK, once the dominant FDI investor in the country, shows disinvestment (on a net basis) in recent years.

BANGLADESH

Overall trends. No reliable and systematic data on FDI are currently available, due to major statistical deficiencies and gaps. The most reliable source are the estimates compiled by UNCTAD and reported in its World Investment Report. According to the UN series, FDI in Bangladesh reached $125 million in 1995, growing from an average of less than $10 million in the previous five years. However, the World Bank's estimate for 1996 suggests a modest increase to $140 million. The FDI approval data from the Board of Investment (BOI) also indicates a rising trend, about 6 times higher than the actual FDI flows—amounting to $720 million equivalent in 1995.

Sectoral patterns. The two Export Processing Zones (EPZs—in Chittagong and Dhaka) have been the main channel for FDI inflows in manufacturing sectors. Since its inception in 1981, a total of 106 projects have been approved (by October 1995) in the Chittagong CEPZ, of which 61 projects were operating, with the total amount of $230 million. Korea is the leading source of FDI in EPZs, with the cumulative total of $56 million in 22 projects, followed by Japan ($46 million in 17 projects), Hong Kong ($16 million) and the United States ($11 million). On the actual investment basis, Japan tops the list with $45 million. The Dhaka EPZ has been in operation since 1993, and has approved a total of $110 million for 36 projects. Korea led the FDI source countries in the Dhaka EPZ also with $42 million, followed by Hong Kong ($27 million) and the United States ($17 million). Among the major sectors attracting FDI in EPZs, textile (including knit and leather) accounts for the bulk of foreign investment, followed by electric/electronic parts and metal products. The recent increases in FDI inflows were largely attributed to service sectors, most notably, telecommunication.

Source countries. FDI in Bangladesh largely originated from neighboring states in Asia. During 1994-95, Malaysia, Singapore, Japan, Korea, and India were the leading sources, accounting for more than 70 percent of the total FDI. The United States and the United Kingdom were the only significant non-Asian direct investors in the country in recent years.

SRI LANKA

Overall trends. FDI in Sri Lanka has grown steadily from less than $50 million a year in the early 1990s to an annual average of almost $200 million since 1993. However, data on approved FDI suggest a continuous decline since the peak of more than $400 million in 1993: to

$190 million in 1995, a 43 percent drop from 1994 and the lowest since 1992. The recent downward trend may be attributed to the unsettling political and social situation, leading to uncertain economic prospects, and the revision in FDI incentive system: this includes the abolition of tax holidays in April 1994—although the new measures introduced in November 1995 reinstated a wide range of preferential treatment for FDI projects.

Sectoral patterns. Roughly 55 percent of new FDI flows since 1993 have been directed to manufacturing sectors, slightly lower than their 60 percent share in the cumulative FDI for 1978-93. Within the manufacturing sectors, the share of textile (clothing and leather goods) has steadily declined, although it remains the single largest sector attracting FDI, accounting for about 30 percent of the total FDI inflows. In contrast, agricultural products and beverage sectors and non-metal mineral products have taken an increasing share, indicating a further sectoral diversification.

Source countries. Based on the approval figures (by end 1995), Singapore led the FDI source economies, with $240 million (equivalent) for 53 projects, including some large projects in telecommunication. Korea was the second leading investor with $184 million for 112 projects, mostly in light manufacturing sectors, followed by Japan with $160 million for 81 projects, predominantly in Japanese clothing, electronic parts, and housing development. This was followed by Hong Kong ($93 million for 58 projects) and the United States ($90 million for 44 projects).

INTRAREGIONAL TRADE

Table III.1 South Asia intraregional exports, 1990-1996

Country	Partner	1990	1991	1992	1993	1994	1995	1996	1990	1991	1992	1993	1994	1995	1996
				(Million US $)								(Share in percent)			
Bangladesh	India	22	23	4	13	24	36	20	1.3	1.4	0.2	0.5	0.9	1.1	0.6
	Nepal	7	12	0	7	14	10	1	0.4	0.7	0.0	0.3	0.5	0.3	0.0
	Pakistan	23	39	30	26	19	26	35	1.4	2.3	1.5	1.1	0.7	0.8	1.0
	Sri Lanka	8	6	11	9	4	11	3	0.5	0.4	0.5	0.4	0.1	0.4	0.1
	South Asia	60	79	46	54	61	84	58	3.6	4.7	2.2	2.4	2.3	2.7	1.7
	World	1672	1687	2037	2277	2652	3129	3343	100	100	100	100	100	100	100
India	Bangladesh	297	325	353	430	521	960	882	1.7	1.8	1.8	2.1	2.2	3.1	2.5
	Nepal	40	77	73	75	85	107	137	0.2	0.4	0.4	0.4	0.3	0.4	0.4
	Pakistan	43	40	52	58	59	70	196	0.2	0.2	0.3	0.3	0.2	0.2	0.6
	Sri Lanka	102	175	231	247	334	383	441	0.6	1.0	1.2	1.2	1.4	1.3	1.3
	South Asia	482	617	709	810	998	1521	1656	2.7	3.4	3.7	3.9	4.1	5.0	4.8
	World	17813	17873	19230	20818	24196	30537	34603	100	100	100	100	100	100	100
Nepal	Bangladesh	1	0	0	0	0	4	5	0.6	0.0	0.1	0.1	0.1	1.1	1.4
	India	14	17	21	17	13	25	33	6.4	6.8	5.9	4.7	3.6	7.7	9.7
	Pakistan	0	4	3	1	0	0	0	0.2	1.5	0.9	0.2	0.1	0.1	0.1
	Sri Lanka	0	0	22	0	0	0	0	0.0	0.0	6.1	0.0	0.0	0.0	0.0
	South Asia	16	21	46	18	13	29	39	7.2	8.3	13.0	4.9	3.8	9.0	11.2
	World	216	257	352	367	350	322	345	100	100	100	100	100	100	100
Pakistan	Bangladesh	103	101	136	105	119	153	109	1.8	1.5	1.9	1.6	1.6	1.9	1.2
	India	49	47	136	53	46	39	41	0.9	0.7	1.9	0.8	0.6	0.5	0.4
	Nepal	1	0	1	0	3	3	6	0.0	0.0	0.0	0.0	0.0	0.0	0.1
	Sri Lanka	69	68	85	57	70	55	80	1.2	1.0	1.2	0.9	1.0	0.7	0.9
	South Asia	222	216	358	216	238	250	236	4.0	3.3	4.9	3.2	3.2	3.1	2.5
	World	5587	6494	7270	6703	7344	7991	9299	100	100	100	100	100	100	100
Sri Lanka	Bangladesh	10	5	7	7	6	10	9	0.5	0.2	0.3	0.3	0.2	0.3	0.2
	India	20	13	12	20	28	35	42	1.1	0.6	0.5	0.7	0.9	0.9	1.0
	Nepal	0	0	1	0	0	0	0	0.0	0.0	0.0	0.0	0.0	0.0	0.0
	Pakistan	32	32	29	35	38	45	40	1.7	1.6	1.2	1.2	1.2	1.2	1.0
	South Asia	63	49	48	63	73	90	92	3.3	2.5	1.9	2.2	2.3	2.4	2.2
	World	1895	1987	2488	2859	3220	3740	4107	100	100	100	100	100	100	100

Source: Direction of Trade Statistics, IMF

Table III.2 South Asia intraregional imports, 1990-1996

Country	Partner	1990	1991	1992	1993	1994	1995	1996	1990	1991	1992	1993	1994	1995	1996
		(Million US $)							(Share in percent)						
Bangladesh	India	170	189	284	380	467	994	1138	4.7	5.5	7.6	9.5	10.1	15.3	16.2
	Nepal	2	0	0	0	1	4	5	0.0	0.0	0.0	0.0	0.0	0.1	0.1
	Pakistan	70	57	88	90	110	138	87	1.9	1.7	2.4	2.2	2.4	2.1	1.2
	Sri Lanka	8	5	6	7	7	11	10	0.2	0.1	0.1	0.2	0.1	0.2	0.1
	South Asia	250	252	378	478	584	1147	1241	6.8	7.4	10.1	11.9	12.7	17.6	17.7
	World	3656	3421	3731	4015	4605	6504	7017	100	100	100	100	100	100	100
India	Bangladesh	15	6	10	13	34	79	42	0.1	0.0	0.0	0.1	0.1	0.2	0.1
	Nepal	15	19	23	19	14	27	36	0.1	0.1	0.1	0.1	0.1	0.1	0.1
	Pakistan	45	58	146	47	47	37	49	0.2	0.3	0.6	0.2	0.2	0.1	0.1
	Sri Lanka	22	12	14	17	31	39	46	0.1	0.1	0.1	0.1	0.1	0.1	0.1
	South Asia	97	94	192	96	126	183	173	0.4	0.5	0.8	0.4	0.5	0.5	0.4
	World	23990	19636	23197	21497	25486	34456	40488	100	100	100	100	100	100	100
Nepal	Bangladesh	8	13	0	8	16	11	1	1.8	2.5	0.1	1.5	2.6	1.5	0.1
	India	43	85	80	83	93	118	150	9.6	17.0	16.8	15.7	15.2	15.7	20.5
	Pakistan	1	1	2	0	4	3	6	0.3	0.1	0.3	0.1	0.6	0.4	0.8
	Sri Lanka	0	0	1	0	0	0	0	0.0	0.0	0.2	0.0	0.0	0.0	0.0
	South Asia	53	98	83	91	113	132	157	11.7	19.6	17.4	17.3	18.3	17.6	21.4
	World	454	500	477	527	614	750	730	100	100	100	100	100	100	100
Pakistan	Bangladesh	38	37	50	38	24	35	36	0.5	0.4	0.5	0.4	0.3	0.3	0.3
	India	46	44	52	67	72	81	212	0.6	0.5	0.6	0.7	0.8	0.7	1.7
	Nepal	0	4	4	1	0	1	0	0.0	0.1	0.0	0.0	0.0	0.0	0.0
	Sri Lanka	37	34	33	41	42	50	45	0.5	0.4	0.4	0.4	0.5	0.4	0.4
	South Asia	121	120	139	147	139	166	292	1.6	1.4	1.5	1.6	1.6	1.4	2.4
	World	7383	8431	9375	9494	8888	11460	12150	100	100	100	100	100	100	100
Sri Lanka	Bangladesh	9	4	15	7	4	13	3	0.3	0.1	0.4	0.2	0.1	0.2	0.0
	India	118	220	307	343	367	422	481	4.5	7.2	8.8	8.6	7.0	6.6	7.1
	Nepal	0	0	24	0	0	0	0	0.0	0.0	0.7	0.0	0.0	0.0	0.0
	Pakistan	51	74	67	55	77	61	88	1.9	2.4	1.9	1.4	1.5	1.0	1.3
	South Asia	178	298	413	405	448	495	572	6.7	9.7	11.9	10.1	8.5	7.8	8.5
	World	2636	3061	3473	4005	5246	6351	6745	100	100	100	100	100	100	100

Source: Direction of Trade Statistics, IMF

Table III.3 South Asia intraregional trade, 1990-1996

Country	Partner	1990	1991	1992	1993	1994	1995	1996	1990	1991	1992	1993	1994	1995	1996
		(Million US $)							(Share in percent)						
Bangladesh	India	192	212	288	393	491	1030	1158	3.6	4.2	5.0	6.2	6.8	10.7	11.2
	Nepal	9	12	1	7	15	14	6	0.2	0.2	0.0	0.1	0.2	0.1	0.1
	Pakistan	93	97	118	116	128	164	122	1.8	1.9	2.1	1.8	1.8	1.7	1.2
	Sri Lanka	16	11	16	16	10	22	13	0.3	0.2	0.3	0.3	0.1	0.2	0.1
	South Asia	310	331	423	532	645	1230	1299	5.8	6.5	7.3	8.5	8.9	12.8	12.5
	World	5328	5108	5768	6292	7257	9633	10360	100	100	100	100	100	100	100
India	Bangladesh	312	330	363	443	555	1038	924	0.7	0.9	0.9	1.0	1.1	1.6	1.2
	Nepal	55	96	96	94	98	135	174	0.1	0.3	0.2	0.2	0.2	0.2	0.2
	Pakistan	88	98	198	105	107	108	245	0.2	0.3	0.5	0.2	0.2	0.2	0.3
	Sri Lanka	124	186	245	264	365	422	487	0.3	0.5	0.6	0.6	0.7	0.6	0.6
	South Asia	579	711	901	905	1125	1703	1829	1.4	1.9	2.1	2.1	2.3	2.6	2.4
	World	41803	37509	42426	42315	49682	64993	75090	100	100	100	100	100	100	100
Nepal	Bangladesh	9	13	1	8	16	15	6	1.4	1.7	0.1	0.9	1.7	1.4	0.5
	India	57	102	101	100	106	143	183	8.5	13.5	12.2	11.2	11.0	13.3	17.0
	Pakistan	2	4	5	1	4	4	6	0.2	0.6	0.6	0.1	0.4	0.3	0.6
	Sri Lanka	0	0	23	0	0	0	0	0.0	0.0	2.7	0.0	0.0	0.0	0.0
	South Asia	68	120	129	109	126	161	195	10.2	15.8	15.6	12.2	13.1	15.0	18.2
	World	670	757	829	894	963	1072	1075	100	100	100	100	100	100	100
Pakistan	Bangladesh	141	138	186	143	143	188	145	1.1	0.9	1.1	0.9	0.9	1.0	0.7
	India	95	91	188	120	118	119	253	0.7	0.6	1.1	0.7	0.7	0.6	1.2
	Nepal	2	5	5	1	4	3	6	0.0	0.0	0.0	0.0	0.0	0.0	0.0
	Sri Lanka	106	102	118	98	112	105	125	0.8	0.7	0.7	0.6	0.7	0.5	0.6
	South Asia	343	336	496	363	377	416	528	2.6	2.2	3.0	2.2	2.3	2.1	2.5
	World	12970	14926	16645	16197	16232	19451	21449	100	100	100	100	100	100	100
Sri Lanka	Bangladesh	19	9	22	14	10	23	12	0.4	0.2	0.4	0.2	0.1	0.2	0.1
	India	138	233	318	363	395	457	523	3.0	4.6	5.3	5.3	4.7	4.5	4.8
	Nepal	0	0	25	0	0	0	0	0.0	0.0	0.4	0.0	0.0	0.0	0.0
	Pakistan	83	106	96	91	115	106	129	1.8	2.1	1.6	1.3	1.4	1.0	1.2
	South Asia	240	347	461	468	520	585	664	5.3	6.9	7.7	6.8	6.1	5.8	6.1
	World	4532	5049	5961	6865	8466	10091	10852	100	100	100	100	100	100	100

Source: Direction of Trade Statistics, IMF

Table III.4 Concessions offered and received by India to/from Bangladesh, Sri Lanka, and Pakistan in SAPTA I & II contained under top 50 products traded during 1995-96 (value in RS1000)

		Concessions offered to			Concessions received from		
Rank	Description	Bangladesh	Pakistan	Sri Lanka	Bangladesh	Pakistan	Sri Lanka
1	Meal of soybean solvent extracted					776236	
3	Grapes dried		68907				
5	Beans-Others		58519				
6	Vegetable seeds for planting NES.					73915*	
7	Other coloring materials					72981	
8	Resin-Gum		33252				
11	Meal of soybean solvent extracted					48539	
11	Copper waste & scrap of copper alloys			21856*			
12	Reactive yellows					43866	
13	Steel bullets						137256
15	Plants-Pine oleoresins			17365*			
16	Betel nut, Whole			17296*			
19	Reactive greens					32099	
20	Reactive oranges					30207	
20	Cotton yarn--Grey						92841
21	Reactive blues					28360	
22	Plants-Other balsam and cleoresins			11939*			
25	Plants-Camoge fruit rind			9557			
26	Plants-Others				140490		
28	Plants-Psyllium husk				11787		
29	Other gum resins			8221*			
30	Reactive voilets					11021	
31	Cotton yarn--Others						70635
32	Licourice roots		4228				
32	Disperse dyes and preparations					10342	
33	Carbon black for rubber industries						69118
33	Articles of apparel & clothing-Surgical			5275*			
36	Accetyl Salicylic acid, its salts					8837	
38	Polyvinyl vhloride (PVC)						61834
39	Printed books-Other	103					
39	In single sheets, whether or not folded		2203				
40	Electorlytic plants or sheets					8332	
41	Artificial flowers	90					
42	Plants--Other natural gums			3384*			
47	Nutmeg-In shell			2792*			
48	Disperse yellow-Others					5221	
49	Nuts, areca			2726*			
50	Black pepper garbled					4994*	

* Indicates concessions exchanged after SAPTA-I.

No concessions were exchanged between India and Nepal in SAPTA-II.

Only one product was offered concession by India to Maldives under SAPTA-II.

There have been no negotiations between India and Bhutan, bilateral trade being free.

Source: I.N. Mukherji (1997)

Table III.5 Number of products offered concessions under SAPTA-II

Favoring offered	Banglades	Bhutan	India	Maldives	Nepal	Pakistan	Sri Lanka	Total
Bangladesh		2	222 (a)	2	26(b)	13	7	272
Bhutan	1				10 (c)	33	3	47
India	513 (c)			1(c)		375	22	911
Maldives	3	9(c)			3(c)		2	8
Nepal	41(d)	38(c)		12(c)		172	14	277
Pakistan	26(c)	10(c)	230		99(c)		21	386
Sri Lanka	16(c)		22	3(c)	4(c)	53	14	112
Total	600	50	474	18	142	646	83	2013

NOTE: Each tariff line is counted as one product. Hence there is some minor discrepancy with the numbers
the numbers listed serially under NSC

(a) According to products listed serially under NSC: 204 products of which 11 for LDC

(b) 16 products listed serially in NSC: of which 11 for LDC

(c) For LDC only

(d) Of which 25 for LDC

Source : I.N. Mukherji (1997)

ANNEX IV.I

THE IMPORTANCE OF TEXTILE AND CLOTHING EXPORTS TO SOUTH ASIAN COUNTRIES

A useful initial indicator of the importance of textiles and clothing exports is provided by their share in a country's total exports. These shares are reported for the four major South Asian countries in Table IV.1.

Table IV.1: Shares of Clothing and Textiles in Total Exports - South Asia Countries

Country	Year	Tex.Fibers (26)	Textile (65)	Clothing (84)	Total(26+65+84)
		(%)	(%)	(%)	(%)
India	1962-1965	3.8	34.5	0.5	38.8
	1966-1970	2.3	27.6	1.1	31.1
	1971-1975	1.8	22.0	3.4	27.2
	1976-1980	1.2	14.2	6.8.	22.2
	1981-1985	1.1	11.8	8.8	21.8
	1986-1990	1.3	11.6	13.1	26.0
	1991-1994	0.7	12.8	15.4	28.8
Pakistan	1962-1965	54.8	23.3	0.3	78.4
	1966-1970	36.1	38.7	0.6	75.4
	1971-1975	17.3	40.0	2.0	59.3
	1976-1980	8.6	37.6	4.1	50.2
	1981-1985	11.7	38.6	7.5	57.8
	1986-1990	13.8	42.6	15.6	72.0
	1991-1994	5.5	49.8	22.3	77.6
Bangladesh	1962-1965	n.a.	n.a.	n.a.	n.a.
	1966-1970	n.a.	n.a.	n.a.	n.a.
	1971-1975	n.a.	n.a.	n.a.	n.a.
	1977-1980	22.2	49.5	n.a.	71.7
	1981-1985	14.5	45.9	6.1	66.5
	1986-1990	7.7	24.3	34.1	66.0
	1991-1993	4.4	16.5	53.8	74.7
Sri Lanka	1962-1965	2.6	0.0	n.a.	2.7
	1966-1970	2.5	0.0	0.2	2.7
	1971-1975	2.8	0.2	0.5	3.4
	1976-1980	2.0	0.2	5.0	7.2
	1981-1985	1.5	0.6	18.8	21.0
	1986-1990	1.2	1.6	31.2	34.0
	1991-1994	0.7	3.2	45.7	49.6
Nepal	1962-1965	n.a.	n.a.	n.a.	n.a.
	1966-1970	n.a.	n.a.	n.a.	n.a.
	1971-1975	n.a.	n.a.	n.a.	n.a.
	1976-1980	22.8	21.9	1.0	45.6
	1981-1985	8.5	24.8	6.0	39.3
	1986-1990	1.8	33.7	25.5	60.9
	1991-1992	0.0	53.8	21.7	75.6

As is evident from the table, fibers, textiles and clothing contribute a very large share of exports from each of the South Asian countries. In recent years, the share has been lowest for India, at 29 percent of total exports and highest for Pakistan, at 78 percent, and Nepal, at 76 percent, Bangladesh, at 75 percent, and Sri Lanka, at 50 percent, both rely extremely heavily on this sector.

India is unusual in having been more dependent upon exports of textiles in the 1960s than it is today. At that stage, its exports were concentrated heavily in the textile sector, while exports of apparel were negligible. The share of textiles in India's exports has fallen to one third of its level in the early 1960s, while clothing exports have risen to over 15 percent of exports in the 1991-94 period.

The continuing dominance of fibers, textiles and clothing in Pakistan's exports masks very substantial changes in the composition of these exports. In the early 1960s, over half of Pakistan's export revenues were derived from exports of raw fibers, a share that fell to 5 percent in the early 1990s. Exports of textile products increased dramatically in importance, to almost half of total exports in 1991-94. Some of these exports consisted of fibers merely transformed into yarn prior to exporting, but yarn exports made up only 18 percent of total exports. The clothing sector expanded very rapidly in the latter part of the 1980s and in the early 1990s, to contribute almost a quarter of the gross value of exports in 1991-94.

In Bangladesh, the share of exports derived from fibers and textiles fell from over 70 percent in the late 1970s to 20 percent in the early 1990s. Apparel exports, by contrast, grew dramatically, coming to contribute over half of total exports in the early 1990s.

In contrast with the other South Asian countries, exports of fibers and textiles have not historically been important in Sri Lanka. Exports of textiles and clothing made up only 3 percent of total exports from Sri Lanka in the late 1960s. The increase in export share to 50 percent has been a recent phenomenon, and is entirely based on increases in the share of apparel exports since around 1980.

A common feature of export growth in South Asian countries has been a dramatic increase in the share of clothing exports, which has occurred partly at the expense of export market share in fibers and apparel. Clearly, there appears to be a marked increase in the internal competitiveness of the clothing sub-sector both relative to other parts of the fiber/textile/clothing complex, and relative to other export sectors. These changes reflect the increasing capital intensity of the spinning and weaving activities over the period under consideration, which has increased the competitiveness of higher income (and more capital-intensive) economies in these sectors, together with the continuing high labor intensity of apparel manufacture. The expansion of the garment sector in these countries also reflects the improvements in transport and communications that have facilitated efficient and timely production of apparel virtually anywhere in the world.

It is illustrative to compare the changes in export share within the South Asian countries with the changes taking place in the currently dominant East Asian exporters, plus Japan, which formerly dominated these markets. Corresponding data on export shares for these economies are presented in Table IV.2.

Table IV.2: The Share of Textile and Clothing Exports in Total Exports - East Asian Countries:

Country	Year	Tex.Fibers(26) (%)	Textiles (65) (%)	Clothing (84) (%)	Total (26+65+84) (%)
Japan	1962-1965	2.1	16.2	3.8	22.1
	1966-1970	1.2	11.0	3.0	15.2
	1971-1975	1.1	6.7	1.1	8.9
	1976-1980	0.6	4.3	0.5	5.4
	1981-1985	0.4	3.4	0.4	4.3
	1986-1990	0.3	2.2	0.3	2.8
	1991-1994	0.3	1.9	0.2	2.4
Hong Kong	1962-1965	0.3	16.9	35.5	52.7
	1966-1970	0.2	13.9	34.9	49.0
	1971-1975	0.0	11.0	36.9	47.9
	1976-1980	0.0	8.1	39.7	47.9
	1981-1985	0.0	6.5	34.0	40.6
	1986-1990	0.0	7.2	32.9	40.1
	1991-1994	0.0	7.4	32.4	39.8
Korea	1962-1965	6.2	11.2	6.2	23.6
	1966-1970	4.9	12.7	21.7	39.2
	1971-1975	2.7	12.3	24.7	39.7
	1976-1980	0.6	12.0	20.2	32.8
	1981-1985	0.3	9.8	16.1	26.2
	1986-1990	0.4	8.8	14.7	23.8
	1991-1994	0.7	10.8	8.3	19.7
Indonesia	1967-1970	0.0	0.1	0.0	0.2
	1971-1975	0.0	0.0	0.0	0.1
	1976-1980	0.0	0.1	0.2	0.4
	1981-1985	0.0	0.6	1.0	1.6
	1986-1990	0.0	3.5	4.6	8.1
	1991-1994	0.1	7.0	8.9	16.0
Thailand	1962-1965	6.0	0.3	0.2	6.5
	1966-1970	7.8	1.1	0.1	9.0
	1971-1975	4.2	3.8	1.7	9.6
	1976-1980	1.1	5.7	3.5	10.2
	1981-1985	0.5	5.3	6.5	12.3
	1986-1990	0.2	4.8	11.8	16.9
	1991-1994	0.4	3.8	11.3	15.5
Taiwan	1962-1965	0.3	10.1	3.4	13.8
	1966-1970	0.5	12.1	9.1	21.7
	1971-1975	0.6	12.0	16.4	29.0
	1976-1980	0.6	9.8	13.5	23.9
	1981-1985	0.6	7.4	12.3	20.3
	1986-1990	0.7	7.9	8.2	16.9
	1991-1994	0.8	9.8	4.4	14.9
China	1962-1965	5.1	18.3	2.8	26.3
	1966-1970	5.7	16.4	3.2	25.3
	1971-1975	5.8	15.2	4.9	25.9
	1976-1980	4.1	15.1	7.4	26.6
	1981-1985	3.3	13.6	12.4	29.3
	1986-1990	2.8	12.6	18.4	33.7
	1991-1994	0.9	7.6	19.9	28.4

Annex IV.I The importance of textile and clothing exports to South Asian countries

Table IV.2 illustrates some important points about the role of textiles and clothing in the development process. As Anderson (1990), has emphasized, textiles and clothing frequently play an important role in the development process, particularly during the early stages of industrialization. As low-income, labor-intensive countries begin to accumulate capital, they move into labor-intensive manufactures such as textiles and apparel. At a later stage of development, they tend to move out of these industries and into a different range of more capital-intensive industries.

The data period covered comes at the very end of this process for Japan. While textiles were important for Japan in the early 1960s, their importance as a source of exports was falling precipitously, creating opportunities for other suppliers such as Hong Kong, the Republic of Korea and Taiwan, China.

In Hong Kong, the share of exports obtained from textiles has fallen continuously, but the share of exports generated by apparel increased until the late 1970s. This share fell to 34 percent in the early 1980s, and has fallen only slightly since that time, possibly because of the very large quotas obtained by Hong Kong under the MFA, and the opportunities for outsourcing at least part of the production process in China.

The data for Korea and Taiwan show the share of clothing in total exports increasing rapidly in the late 1960s and 1970s, but subsequently declining rapidly. This decline would have been even faster except for the sizable export quotas built up by these countries, which provide preferential access to the high-priced MFA importing markets. The share of clothing in total exports peaked in the early 1970s at 25 percent in Korea and 16.4 percent in Taiwan, China, that is at export shares comparable with India and Pakistan today, but well below the export shares seen historically in Hong Kong, or currently in Bangladesh and Sri Lanka. Interestingly, the share of textiles in the exports of Korea and Taiwan, China increased during the 1970s, before falling substantially in the 1980s. During the early 1990s, the export shares of textiles in these countries actually began to rise again, possibly reflecting a combination of the increasing capital intensity of these industries.

The importance of the clothing sector increased dramatically in Indonesia, Thailand and China during the 1980s and early 1990s, with these exports increasing to around 10 percent of total exports in Indonesia and Thailand and to around 20 percent in China. The experience of the textile sectors in these countries was considerably more diverse, with textiles gaining export market share substantially in Indonesia, but declining in Thailand and China, over this period.

Because the importance of textiles and clothing in world markets has changed substantially over time, simple comparisons of today's export shares in South Asia with those observed in East Asia during earlier decades are likely to be misleading as an indicator of the relative strength of these industries. The index of Revealed Comparative Advantage mitigates this problem by dividing the share of the particular category of exports from a particular country by the share of that good in total world exports. Indexes of Revealed Comparative Advantage (RCA) are presented in Table IV.3 for the South Asian countries for the period since 1962, and in Table IV.4 for the East Asian economies over the longest period for which data are available.

Table IV.3: Revealed Comparative Advantage - South Asia

Country	Year	Tex.Yarn(26)	Textile(65)	Clothing(84)	65+84	26+65+84
India	1962-1965	1.2	6.7	0.3	5.2	3.9
	1966-1970	1.0	6.1	0.6	4.5	3.5
	1971-1975	1.1	5.6	1.8	4.3	3.6
	1976-1980	1.1	4.7	3.4	4.2	3.6
	1981-1985	1.2	4.2	4.0	4.0	3.7
	1986-1990	1.8	3.6	4.3	3.9	3.7
	1991-1994	1.3	4.1	4.4	4.2	4.0
Pakistan	1962-1965	16.9	4.5	0.2	3.5	7.9
	1966-1970	15.4	8.6	0.3	6.1	8.6
	1971-1975	11.0	10.4	1.1	7.2	8.0
	1976-1980	8.2	12.4	2.0	8.3	8.2
	1981-1985	13.2	13.6	3.4	9.2	9.8
	1986-1990	17.4	13.4	5.1	9.3	10.2
	1991-1994	10.0	15.8	6.4	10.9	10.8
Bangladesh	1962-1965	n.a.	n.a.	n.a.	n.a.	n.a.
	1966-1970	n.a.	n.a.	n.a.	n.a.	n.a.
	1971-1975	n.a.	n.a.	n.a.	n.a.	n.a.
	1977-1980	20.9	16.5	0.0	10.0	11.8
	1981-1985	16.1	16.3	2.6	10.4	11.2
	1986-1990	9.8	7.6	11.0	9.3	9.4
	1991-1993	8.1	5.3	15.4	0.0	10.5
Sri Lanka	1962-1965	0.8	0.0	0.0	0.0	0.3
	1966-1970	1.1	0.0	0.0	0.0	0.3
	1971-1975	1.9	0.0	0.3	0.1	0.5
	1976-1980	1.8	0.0	2.5	1.1	1.2
	1981-1985	1.7	0.2	8.5	3.9	3.5
	1986-1990	1.5	0.5	10.2	5.2	4.8
Nepal	1962-1965	n.a.	n.a.	n.a.	n.a.	n.a.
	1966-1970	n.a.	n.a.	n.a.	n.a.	n.a.
	1971-1975	n.a.	n.a.	n.a.	n.a.	n.a.
	1976-1980	20.8	7.2	0.5	4.5	7.4
	1981-1985	9.4	8.7	2.6	6.1	6.6
	1986-1990	2.3	10.7	8.3	9.5	8.7
	1991-1992	0.10	17.2	6.3	11.5	10.5

From the data presented in Table IV.3, it is clear that the RCA's currently observed for the total of fibers, textiles and clothing in Pakistan and Bangladesh are high relative to the peak levels reached in the East Asian exporters. In Pakistan, this reflects high RCAs at each stage, particularly in textiles. In Bangladesh, RCAs are very high for garment production, and in India, in both textiles and clothing. By contrast, Sri Lanka has an RCA of over 13 in clothing, and RCAs of around unity in fibers and textiles.

Table IV.4: Revealed Comparative Advantage - East Asia

Country	Year	Tex.Yarn(26)	Textile(65)	Clothing(84)	65+84	26+65+84
Japan	1899	n.a.	n.a.	n.a.	1.5	n.a.
	1913	n.a.	n.a.	n.a.	2.6	n.a.
	1929	n.a.	n.a.	n.a.	2.9	n.a.
	1937	n.a.	n.a.	n.a.	4.1	n.a.
	1954-1956	n.a.	n.a.	n.a.	5.5	n.a.
	1962-1965	0.7	3.1	2.5	3.0	2.2
	1966-1970	0.5	2.4	1.6	2.2	1.7
	1971-1975	0.7	1.7	0.5	1.3	1.2
	1976-1980	0.6	1.4	0.2	0.9	0.9
	1981-1985	0.5	1.2	0.2	0.8	0.7
	1986-1990	0.4	0.7	0.0	0.4	0.4
	1991-1994	0.5	0.6	0.0	0.3	0.3
Hong Kong	1954-1956	n.a.	n.a.	n.a.	5.4	n.a.
	1962-1965	0.0	3.2	24.0	7.8	5.3
	1966-1970	0.0	3.0	19.3	7.4	5.4
	1971-1975	0.0	2.7	18.3	8.6	6.1
	1976-1980	0.0	2.6	20.2	9.0	7.7
	1981-1985	0.0	2.3	16.2	8.1	6.9
	1986-1990	0.0	2.3	11.5	6.4	5.9
	1991-1994	0.0	2.4	9.5	6.0	5.6
Korea	1962-1965	1.9	2.2	4.0	2.6	2.4
	1966-1970	2.1	2.8	11.3	5.4	4.5
	1971-1975	1.6	3.2	12.4	6.3	5.3
	1976-1980	0.5	4.0	10.1	6.4	5.3
	1981-1985	0.3	3.5	7.4	5.2	4.4
	1986-1990	0.5	2.8	4.8	3.8	3.4
	1991-1994	1.3	3.4	2.4	2.9	2.7
Indonesia	1962	0.0	0.0	0.0	0.0	0.0
	1967-1970	0.0	0.0	0.0	0.0	0.0
	1971-1975	0.0	0.0	0.0	0.0	0.0
	1976-1980	0.0	0.0	0.1	0.0	0.0
	1981-1985	0.0	0.2	0.4	0.3	0.3
	1986-1990	0.0	1.1	1.5	1.3	1.2
	1991-1994	0.2	2.2	2.5	2.4	2.2
Thailand	1962-1965	1.9	0.0	0.1	0.0	0.7
	1966-1970	3.3	0.2	0.0	0.2	1.0
	1971-1975	2.5	1.0	0.9	1.0	1.3
	1976-1980	1.0	1.9	1.7	1.8	1.7
	1981-1985	0.5	1.9	2.9	2.3	2.1
	1986-1990	0.3	1.5	3.8	2.7	2.4
	1991-1994	0.7	1.2	3.3	2.3	2.2
Taiwan	1962-1965	0.0	2.3	2.5	2.4	1.4
	1966-1970	0.2	3.0	5.2	3.7rn	2.6
	1971-1975	0.3	3.3	7.9	5.0	4.0
	1976-1980	0.5	3.3	6.0	4.5	3.8
	1981-1985	0.7	2.8	5.1	3.9	3.4
	1986-1990	0.9	2.5	2.5	2.5	2.3
	1991-1994	1.2	3.1	1.2	2.0	2.0
China	1962-1965	1.3	4.2	2.1	3.7	2.7
	1966-1970	2.4	4.0	1.9	3.4	3.1
	1971-1975	3.5	4.1	2.3	3.5	3.5
	1976-1980	3.8	5.1	3.3	4.3	4.2
	1981-1985	3.8	5.2	5.1	5.2	4.9
	1986-1990	3.3	4.0	5.4	4.8	4.6
	1991-1994	1.4	2.4	5.2	4.0	3.8

Table IV.4 shows that RCAs in Pakistan and Bangladesh are higher than has historically been observed in East Asia. However, the RCAs for clothing of 15 for Bangladesh and 13 for Sri Lanka are well below the peak rates observed in Hong Kong, and in the same order of magnitude as the peak rate of 12 observed in Korea. The RCA of 4 currently observed in India is still considerably below the 5.5 reported for Japan at its peak in the mid 1950s. Clearly, these comparisons are consistent with the clothing sector in South Asia still having considerable scope to expand its contribution to exports if domestic and external policy constraints are relaxed sufficiently to allow this to occur.

Table IV.5: Shares of Exports Going to the Quota Markets - South Asia

Country	Year	Textiles (%)	Clothing (%)
India	1962-1965	49.9	29.3
	1966-1970	55.3	19.9
	1971-1975	46.7	51.8
	1976-1980	51.9	72.5
	1981-1985	46.1	71.8
	1986-1990	56.4	77.2
	1991-1994	53.9	78.5
Pakistan	1962-1965	31.2	41.6
	1966-1970	34.6	48.7
	1971-1975	30.3	66.7
	1976-1980	38.2	67.3
	1981-1985	32.7	62.0
	1986-1990	42.2	81.1
	1991-1994	37.5	86.5
Bangladesh	1977-1980	37.0	n.a.
	1981-1985	34.2	97.6
	1986-1990	37.1	97.8
	1991-1993	40.9	98.2
Sri Lanka	1962-1965	29.3	n.a.
	1966-1970	11.2	n.a.
	1971-1975	28.7	29.2
	1976-1980	60.9	78.5
	1981-1985	59.7	96.0
	1986-1990	68.2	97.0
	1991-1994	70.4	96.5
Nepal	1962-1965	n.a.	n.a.
	1966-1970	n.a.	n.a.
	1971-1975	n.a.	n.a.
	1976-1980	74.6	69.1
	1981-1985	57.4	78.7
	1986-1990	67.8	97.8
	1991-1992	85.4	98.7

Note: The MFA quota markets are the current EU-15, the United States, Canada and Norway.

Data on the share of exports of textiles and clothing exports directed to quota markets are presented in Table IV.5 for South Asian countries and Table IV.6 for East Asian comparators. In general, the higher the share of exports directed towards protected, quota markets, the less restricted is the exporter relative to its supply capacity. Tightly restricted, low-cost exporters are forced to divert a large share of their exports to non-restricted markets. By contrast, exporters with large quotas are likely to focus their attention on the relatively high returns available in the quota markets. Of course, these relationships may be affected by other influences on the pattern and direction of trade, such as transport cost differentials and historical ties with particular countries. The data presented in Table IV.5 make it clear that there are considerable differences between the four major South Asian countries in the direction of their exports. The share of India's textile exports directed to the quota markets has remained relatively stable at around

50 percent, while the share of its apparel exports directed to these markets has increased considerably, to over 78 percent. In Pakistan, the share of textile exports directed to the developed country quota markets has increased from 31 to 37 percent, while the share of apparel exports directed to these markets has more than doubled, from 41 to 86 percent.

For Sri Lanka and Bangladesh, the picture is even more striking, with virtually all of their exports of clothing directed towards the quota markets. Sri Lanka faces quota restrictions in both of the major MFA markets (the EU and the USA) but it appears that exporting to these markets remains more profitable than exporting to unrestricted markets, even after taking into account the implicit taxes imposed by the MFA quotas. Bangladesh faces quotas in the USA, but not in the EU, and these two markets provide enough market access at favorable prices to meet the total supply from Bangladesh.

Table IV.6: Shares of Exports Going to the Quota Markets - East Asia

Country	Year	Textile (%)	Clothing (%)
Hong Kong	1962-1965	55.8	79.9
	1966-1970	55.6	84.2
	1971-1975	48.2	83.5
	1976-1980	41.1	82.4
	1981-1985	29.9	82.1
	1986-1990	22.7	85.7
	1991-1994	15.7	86.4
Korea	1962-1965	62.4	94.8
	1966-1970	36.2	79.2
	1971-1975	26.5	70.5
	1976-1980	20.7	71.3
	1981-1985	23.2	72.1
	1986-1990	23.9	66.1
	1991-1994	14.2	60.2
Indonesia	1967-1970	14.4	n.a.
	1971-1975	12.3	73.0
	1976-1980	28.1	51.8
	1981-1985	34.0	79.0
	1986-1990	37.5	80.1
	1991-1994	29.3	64.3
Thailand	1962-1965	36.5	10.6
	1966-1970	18.3	58.8
	1971-1975	20.6	90.1
	1976-1980	42.2	78.9
	1981-1985	42.1	71.0
	1986-1990	44.7	55.7
	1991-1994	39.0	49.3
Taiwan, China	1962-1965	22.4	86.1
	1966-1970	18.0	87.8
	1971-1975	25.4	81.0
	1976-1980	21.7	75.2
	1981-1985	22.4	75.8
	1986-1990	19.4	77.6
	1991-1994	11.4	81.6
China	1962-1965	16.7	15.8
	1966-1970	17.0	22.9
	1971-1975	19.3	21.6
	1976-1980	23.3	33.6
	1981-1985	25.8	43.6
	1986-1990	22.6	42.7
	1991-1994	20.9	40.1

For comparison, data on the export shares of East Asian developing countries are presented in Table IV.6. It appears that the concentration of exports from the East Asian exporters on the MFA quota markets is generally considerably lower than is currently the case in South Asia. Only Hong Kong and Taiwan, China ship over 80 percent of their exports to the MFA importing countries. The other countries are sufficiently competitive that their producers find it profitable to produce substantial quantities for export to the less lucrative non-MFA export markets. Korea and Indonesia ship almost 40 percent of their exports to non-quota markets, while Thailand sends over 50 percent of its exports to non-quota markets. China sends sixty percent of its exports to these markets.

A useful indicator of the extent to which quotas restrict exports is provided by the quota utilization rate. In a theoretical model, the quotas would be expected to fill whenever there are any exports directed to non-quota markets. However, this is not necessarily the case in practice since the quotas are broken up into relatively finely specified categories. Some of these quotas may go unfilled while others are tightly bind tightly. However, in general, the more restrictive the quotas the higher their utilization rate is likely to be.

Data on the quota utilization rates in the United States market for particular exporters are presented in Table IV.7. From these data, it appears that the South Asian countries may have been relatively tightly restricted in the United States market during recent years. In 1992 and 1993, in particular, India, Pakistan and Bangladesh all filled their overall quotas close to 100 percent. Such high rates are extremely difficult to achieve given the fineness of the product classifications, and the probability that demand will be relatively weak for some product lines in any given year. Typically, countries only achieve such high overall quota utilization levels by utilizing options such as carry-forward in some years, which reduces their allowable exports in subsequent years. India's quota utilization rate fell to 93 percent in 1994, while that for Pakistan fell dramatically, to below 70 percent, presumably reflecting severe supply constraints within Pakistan.

The quota utilization rate in Sri Lanka was 80 percent in 1994, still well above the overall average utilization rate of 70 percent. Nepal's quota utilization rate has trended upwards since the mid 1980s, but has generally been below the rate applying in the other South Asian countries.

Table IV.7. Utilization of textile and clothing quotas in the United States Market.

	India	Pakistan	Bangladesh	Sri Lanka	Nepal	Hong Kong	Korea	Indonesia	Thailand	Taiwan, China	China	Total
1981	30	79 .		92 .		81	88 .		50	93	95	67
1982	10	61 .		81 .		92	95	100	64	103	71	64
1983	95	75 .		94 .		96	90	97	82	95	101	77
1984	96	71 .		94 .		86	86	89	90	91	96	67
1985	88	69 .		60 .		84	91	83	83	90	87	75
1986	95	58	94	95	56	93	88	96	83	86	99	80
1987	98	82	95	86	52	88	91	92	85	86	94	80
1988	82	76	90	75	42	84	82	93	78	74	85	69
1989	73	81	90 .		27	88	85	95	89	77	93	71
1991 .		93	82	91 .		.		93 .		.		77
1992	99	100	100	77	71 .		75	90	92	84	99	87
1993	99	97	100	80	71 .		67	95	96	74	90	73
1994	93	69	99	80	76 .		74	95	88	82	94	70

Source: MFA Database, International Trade Division, World Bank. Data obtained from the U.S. Dept. of Commerce.

THE BASELINE SIMULATIONS: ASSUMPTIONS AND METHODOLOGY

The simulations in this study are undertaken using the GTAP model of the global economy. The GTAP model is a relatively standard computable general equilibrium (CGE) model of the world economy developed and maintained at Purdue University with support from a consortium of national and international agencies. The model is comprehensively documented in Hertel (1996) and is regularly used for policy analysis and projections by a wide range of national and international organizations. Details on the project, the database and the underlying model are available on the World Wide Web.[1] The base year for Version 3 of the model, the version used in this analysis, was 1992, and all of the analysis was undertaken from this base year. The projections scenario is based on the World Bank's macroeconomic projections, and estimates and projections of policies and costs affecting world trade in goods.

Projections of factor accumulation and economic growth are based on World Bank's macroeconomic, labor force, populations and human capital growth assumptions. The macroeconomic projections underlying the policy simulations to 2005 are in Table IV.8.

Table IV.8 The Growth Rates Underlying the Projections to 2005
percent per year

	Population	Labor Force	Physical Capital	Human Capital	TFP	GDP
North America	1.1	1.3	3.3	3.3	0.2	2.8
EU15	0.1	0.1	2.5	2.6	0.8	2.5
Japan	0.2	-0.2	4.3	2.8	0.3	2.7
Other OECD	0.8	0.9	2.8	4.0	0.4	2.8
Newly Industrializing Economies	0.8	1.0	8.8	6.2	1.1	6.7
Hong-Kong	0.5	0.6	8.8	4.8	-0.6	5.3
China	0.9	1.2	10.1	3.5	3.6	9.6
Indonesia	1.4	0.0	7.8	9.9	1.6	7.0
Malaysia, Philippines, Thailand	1.8	2.3	9.1	6.5	0.2	7.5
India	1.7	2.1	5.7	5.8	0.8	5.4
Rest of South Asia	2.2	2.9	5.0	6.0	0.4	4.7
Brazil	1.3	2.1	3.7	5.4	0.5	4.0
Rest of Latin America	1.6	2.1	3.7	7.1	0.1	3.6
Sub Saharan Africa	2.8	3.1	1.1	7.2	0.6	3.3
Economies in Transition	0.3	0.5	0.7	5.4	0.0	1.6
Middle East and North Africa	2.5	3.2	2.6	8.0	-2.9	0.4
Rest of World	1.8	2.1	4.7	7.4	-0.6	3.6

Assumptions on the growth in the stock of skilled labor are based on independent World Bank projections. The rates of total factor productivity (tfp) growth are generally assumed to be

---

[1] See www.agecon.purdue.edu/gtap.

uniform across sectors within each region, except for primary agriculture, where tfp growth rate is specified to be 0.7 percent per year higher (to take into account new empirical evidence, see Martin and Mitra 1996).

In the simulations to 2005, industrial countries reduce their average tariffs on manufactures from 4.1 to 2.6 percent in line with their Uruguay Round commitments, while developing countries lower their barriers on these products from an average of 19 percent to 14 percent (Abreu 1996; Finger, Ingco and Reincke 1996). Modest liberalization of agricultural barriers is included, as is the increase in the growth rates of MFA quotas agreed under the Uruguay Round (Martin and Winters 1996). China is assumed to join the WTO with its current offers on tariff reductions.[2] All of the South Asian countries reduce their protection in line with the reductions in protection between India's 1991 tariff regime and its 1998 tariff regime.

Table IV.9 illustrates some of the economic growth assumptions for the period between 1992 and 2020. The scenario assumes a strong GDP growth for the developing countries as a group (5.4% per year, relative to 2.9% in the high income countries). India and the rest of South Asia are expected to grow by 5.8% and 5.2% a year respectively. The macro projections are combined with the assumption that the trend of policy reform begun during the 1990s continues. Developing country protection is assumed to decline to the current level in industrial countries, and integration to be stimulated by a 2 percent annual decline in transport costs (see Global Economic Prospects 1997). Table IV.10 reports trade growth rates and market shares during the period 1992-2020.

---

[2] These estimates are based on the methodology used by Bach, Martin and Stevens (1996) and result in China's weighted average tariffs declining from 31.2 in 1992 to 16.2 in 2005, assuming full implementation of the tariff bindings, but no other changes in applied rates from the 1996 tariff schedule. This understates the likely liberalization in China, which has announced, in the context of the APEC process, its intention to reduce its applied rates from an unweighted average of 23 percent in 1996 to 15 percent by 2000. The full details of this liberalization are not yet available, however.

Table IV.9 World growth and shares in GDP, 1992 and 2020

	Annual Average % Growth						% Share of World	
	Real GDP 1			Capital Stock	TFP		Real GDP 1	
	1974-82	1982-92	1992-95	'92-2020	'92-2020	'92-2020	1992	2020
World	2.6	3.0	2.4	2.9	3.6	0.5	100.0	100.0
High Income	2.3	3.1	2.2	2.5	3.3	0.3	84.2	70.9
OECD	2.2	2.9	2.0	2.4	3.1	0.3	81.5	66.7
NIEs 2	8.0	8.7	7.4	4.9	6.0	1.3	2.3	3.8
Hong Kong	7.7	9.3	7.8	4.0	4.0	1.1	0.3	0.4
Developing Countries	3.7	2.6	3.1	5.4	6.0	1.3	15.7	29.1
Big 5	4.4	2.7	3.3	5.8	7.2	1.7	7.8	16.1
China	6.5	10.3	12.5	7.0	9.5	2.2	1.4	3.9
India	4.4	5.4	5.5	5.8	6.7	1.9	1.0	2.1
Brazil	4.3	1.8	4.8	4.6	4.6	1.1	1.7	2.5
Indonesia	6.8	7.1	7.6	6.9	6.9	1.9	0.6	1.5
Econ.in Transition3	3.8	-0.7	-5.4	5.5	7.0	1.7	3.2	6.0
ASEAN (3)	6.3	5.6	7.7	7.1	6.7	2.0	0.8	2.4
Rest of S.Asia	5.3	5.2	4.0	5.2	5.7	1.4	0.3	0.6
Rest of L.America	3.0	2.0	2.2	4.2	4.0	0.9	2.1	2.9
S.Saharan Africa	2.2	2.0	2.1	4.2	3.4	0.8	1.2	1.7
M.East/N.Africa	2.2	2.0	2.1	4.2	4.1	0.3	2.3	3.1
Rest of World	3.3	2.4	2.6	5.6	5.8	1.4	1.2	2.3

1 Constant 1992 US dollars using market exchange rates. 2 Korea, Singapore and Taiwan, China.
3 Due to data limitations economies in transition are modeled as a group.
Source: GTAP Database, World Bank data and staff estimates

Table IV.10 Trade growth and market shares, 1992-2020
(exports and imports in constant 1992 US$)

	Exports			Imports		
	% Growth	% Share of World		% Growth	% Share of World	
	1992-202	1992	2020	1992-202	1992	2020
World	5.5	100	100	5.3	100	100
High Income	4	76.5	51.6	4.3	74.3	56.6
OECD	3.5	67.8	40.4	4	65.3	45.3
NIEs	6.5	7.4	9.7	6.3	7.2	9.4
Hong Kong	6	1.3	1.5	5.7	1.8	1.9
Developing C	[8.1]	23.5	48.4	7.3	25.7	43.4
Big 5	8.9	9	22	8.5	8.7	20.1
China	10	3	9.8	10.2	2.8	9.9
India	12	0.7	3.9	11	0.8	3.2
Brazil	7.2	1.2	1.9	6.8	0.9	1.3
Indonesia	8.8	1.1	2.7	7.8	0.9	1.8
Econ.in Tra	6.2	3	3.6	5.9	3.4	3.9
ASEAN (3)	9.6	2.8	8.4	8.6	3	7
Rest of S.Asi	8	0.5	0.9	6.8	0.6	0.8
Rest of L.Am	6.7	2.8	3.9	5.4	3.5	3.5
S.Saharan Af	6.7	1.7	2.4	5.3	2.1	2.1
M.East/N.Afri	6.4	5.2	6.6	5.4	5.9	6
Rest of Worl	9.4	1.5	4.2	8.1	1.9	3.9

Source: GTAP Database, World Bank data and staff estimates